You matter, always.

♡ Dayna

Bake it Till You Make it LLC presents

A Unifying Blend: A compilation of recipes and stories to celebrate all that makes us human
by Dayna Altman

Dedication

In loving memory of Abbey Wolf, who was lost to suicide on November 7, 2020.

I can confidently say that being introduced to the Wolf family was not an accident.

I feel humbled to not only share Abbey's story in *A Unifying Blend* but also to dedicate this book to her.

If you are reading this and you or someone you know may be experiencing a mental health emergency or crisis, there is free and confidential help available 24/7/365 days. Please call 1-800-273-8255 or text "HOME" to 741-741.

Abbey, I wish we could have met but ever since learning about you, I have been carrying you in my heart as I continue this important mental health work. Whether it is in writing, speaking, or baking, you will not be forgotten and it is an honor to dedicate this book to you and your family!

Acknowledgments

A huge thank you to Jason SonDu Taglieri for designing and organizing this book, thank you for being my partner in all things Bake it Till You Make it!

Appreciation to Hannah Little for copyediting, you are amazing!

Brenna Stewart Photography, from the front and back cover to the food photography, your amazing work ties the whole thing together, thank you!

To all the contributors, thank you for allowing me to share your stories. Your brave, vulnerable and authentic stories are changing the world!

Table of Contents

IT

you make it

Foreword

You are not alone.

A simple four-word phrase that has become not only the anthem of the Broadway musical *Dear Evan Hansen,* the tag line for countless mental health organizations, and the caption of so many of my Instagram posts, but it is also at the center of the mental health movement.

If you truly think about it, it couldn't be more true! According to Google, there are over 7 billion people on the planet—a number with so many zeros I can't comprehend—so I constantly question, why is it so many of us feel alone?

I think if we could answer this question, so much human suffering would subside, or at least I know a lot of mine would. Being alone and/or feeling alone is one of the scariest things I have faced and continue to face. I think this was quite obvious to my family early on, when my younger sister ended up being the person to babysit me growing up because I was too afraid... of murders and intruders, yes, but of my own mind just the same. Later, when I was a sophomore in college and took a medical leave from school because of unrelenting suicidal ideation and planning, I wasn't ever in the house alone, but I certainly was in my mind. I can remember going to Michaels, the craft store, and buying a sketchbook during this time and drawing pictures of my mind alone in a prison cell. Not just because I couldn't escape the thoughts but because of how truly alone I felt in my own personal "cell."

I want to say over the last ten years, things have felt less lonely, and I would say I have more days I feel connected than not. However, I have learned sometimes choosing my mental health means being left out of things. Protecting my own energy and mind has at times meant sitting out events and in a FOMO (fear of missing out) based society, it isn't always the easy choice. Nevertheless, I have always believed choosing my mental health over anything else is brave.

In fact, I don't think there is a more courageous thing to do than battle your brain. Although I would venture to say most people who do battle their brain daily didn't choose this battle, as you will read here, the journey has shaped us into kinder and more thoughtful, complex, and beautiful people than we may have ever imagined we could be.

My mental illness has taken so much away from me, but I think it has given more than it has taken: a career, a passion, meaningful relationships and mental health advocacy, entrepreneurship and Bake it Till You Make it LLC (and this lights me up inside to the point the glow on my face is contagious!).

I have realized when I am at my lowest, the beautiful art of advocacy saves me every time. I started Bake it Till You Make it LLC when I was in a place of ultimate "aloneness" and despair. This was in the midst of a depressive episode, surviving a car accident and the end of my first long-term relationship. And yet the first cookbook-turned-organization-turned-community brought me not only out but also back to life and continues to each time I struggle. Living with OCD, depression, and being in recovery from an eating disorder and a sexual assault is like a full-time job, but the way I have learned my story can inspire others gets me up each day even when I feel like I can't face another one.

When creating another resilience cookbook came to the forefront of my metaphorical plate, I knew I wanted it to be centered around this concept of humanness, because at the end of the day, no matter how alone we feel, there are billions of other people experiencing the same pain, joy, thrill, excitement, disappointment, and heartache alongside each of us. When I started speaking publicly and giving presentations about my story, my journey, and my life, I felt I was unique. And yet every time I am cleaning up after a presentation, there is a long line that forms behind me of other humans who may not have the same story but have felt the exact same way and feel seen because somebody else is talking about it.

So be brave, speak up, share, and celebrate in community. We all have our own stories, but we all live in unison with one another. We all face something, whether it is in our brains, bodies, or otherwise, so why feel so alone? This book will give you over 30 reasons to believe you are not!

It has been such an honor sitting with these stories, understanding them, reading them, editing them, and getting up each day because of them. I hope when you put down this book you are just as inspired as I have been through this process. At the end of the day, we are all just human.

We All Have Mental Health

While we can all agree everyone has physical health, recognizing we all have mental health is a little bit more difficult for some. It may be helpful to think about mental health and well-being as a spectrum and we all fall somewhere different on that continuum. Where we fall may also change as often as day-to-day or moment-to-moment, and that is okay. The more we recognize and normalize mental health in all aspects of the spectrum, the better we can understand that we are not alone.

	HEALTHY	REACTING	INJURED	ILL
	Normal Functioning	Common & Reversible Distress	Significant Functional Impairment	Clinical Disorder. Severe & Persistent Functional Impairment
MOOD	Normal mood fluctuations Calmness and the ability to take things in stride	Being irritable or impatient Being nervous Being sad or overwhelmed	Anger Anxiety Pervasive sadness or hopelessness	Angry outbursts or aggression Excessive anxiety or panic attacks Depression or suicidal thoughts
ATTITUDE	A good sense of humour Good performance Being in control	Expressing displaced sarcasm Procrastination Forgetfulness	A negative attitude Poor performance or workaholic behaviour Poor concentration or decisions	Excessive insubordination An inability to perform duties, control behaviour or concentrate
SLEEP	Normal sleep patterns Few sleep difficulties	Having trouble sleeping Having intrusive thoughts Having nightmares	Restless or disturbed sleep Recurrent images or nightmares	An inability to fall asleep or stay asleep Sleeping too much or too little
PHYSICAL HEALTH	Being physically well Having a good energy level	Having muscle tension or headaches Having low energy	Increased aches and pains Increased fatigue	Physical illnesses Constant fatigue
ACTIVITY	Being physically and socially active	Decreased activity or socializing	Avoidance Withdrawal	Not going out or not answering phone
HABITS	Limited or no alcohol use or gambling.	Regular but controlled alcohol use or gambling.	Increased alcohol use or hard-to-control gambling	Alcohol or gambling addiction Other addictions

ACTIONS TO TAKE AT EACH PHASE OF THE CONTINUUM

Focus on task at hand Break problems into manageable chunks Identify and nurture support systems Maintain healthy lifestyle	Recognize limits Identify and minimize stressors Engage in healthy coping strategies Get adequate food, rest, and exercise	Identify and understand own signs of distress Seek social support and talk with someone instead of withdrawing Seek help	Seek consultation as needed Follow health care provider recommendations Regain physical and mental health

While we know everyone has mental health, mental health is not seen or experienced the same way across all communities, cultures, and identities. Learn more about the way some communities are facing different challenges below through examples of data pulled from NAMI: National Alliance on Mental Illness fact sheets. Note, these are just some examples of many views on mental health.

Lack of Acknowledgement in the Black Community

13.4% of the US population identify as Black or African American and 16% of that total reported having mental illness this year; that's about 7 million people.

According to a study conducted by Ward, Wiltshire, Detry, and Brown in 2013, people who identify as Black and/or African American generally hold beliefs related to mental health stigma, which in turn affects their coping behaviors and acknowledgement of psychological problems. Participants in the study stated that if they were to suffer from anxiety or depression, their peers would believe they were "crazy."

Barriers to Treatment in the Latinx Community

Latinx communities show similar vulnerability to mental illness as the general population, but they face disparities in both access to and quality of treatment. More than half of Hispanic young adults ages 18-25 with serious mental illness may not receive treatment at all. This is in part due to cultural acceptance of mental health, language barriers that exist in treatment, and at times lack of insurance coverage.

Prevalance in the LGBTQIA Community

4.5% of the US population identifies as lesbian, gay, or bisexual. Of those, over 39% reported having mental illness this past year.

LGBTQIA teens are six times more likely to experience symptoms of depression than non-LGBTQIA identifying teens.

LGBTQIA youth are more than twice as likely to feel suicidal and over four times as likely to attempt suicide compared to heterosexual youth.

48% of transgender adults report that they have considered suicide in the last year, compared to 4% of the overall US population.

The Journey to Self Love

Author's Voice:

On my second day of eating disorder treatment, I purchased a bright green "I am Enough" bracelet from a seller on Etsy. Although this $12 purchase may have seemed like a small transaction, this was my first step to buying into the idea that I could love myself someday.

From as early as I can remember, I was scribbling the words "I hate me" on the corner of my school notebooks and folders. There was always an innate disgust I had for myself; I hated my body and I didn't understand my feelings. I would feel so sad all the time. I wanted something "bad to happen" to justify those big sad feelings and felt embarrassed I had them; I hated that. I could never catch my breath from the anxious thoughts and repetitive compulsive behaviors; I hated that. I wanted to be as thin as possible so maybe I could at least like my body, but anyone who has dealt with an eating disorder before knows no matter how low the number gets on the scale, it is never enough. The journey to self-love felt impossible from here, so I worked toward self-tolerance.

There was not one moment that helped me let go of my self-hatred. I do know the years of mental health hospital treatment and therapy helped me understand that I could, in fact, communicate my feelings and that those feelings were valid and justified because I felt them, end of story. I also came to recognize and see that my big feelings are one of the most beautiful parts about me; it allows me to connect with others deeply and that is really special.

Self-love did not show up when I thought it would, though. I always thought it would come with an accomplishment: a new job, a book, an award, a milestone. And while those moments are special in their own right, the feeling is fleeting. Rather, to come to a place of sustained love and acceptance, there is an innate knowing that one is enough simply because they exist. And while I know that to be true, I am still working towards it... That's the thing about self-love: it is a journey and one that does not have just one destination. This chapter of the book feels so important for this reason. Self-love looks different for everyone—what will it look like for you?

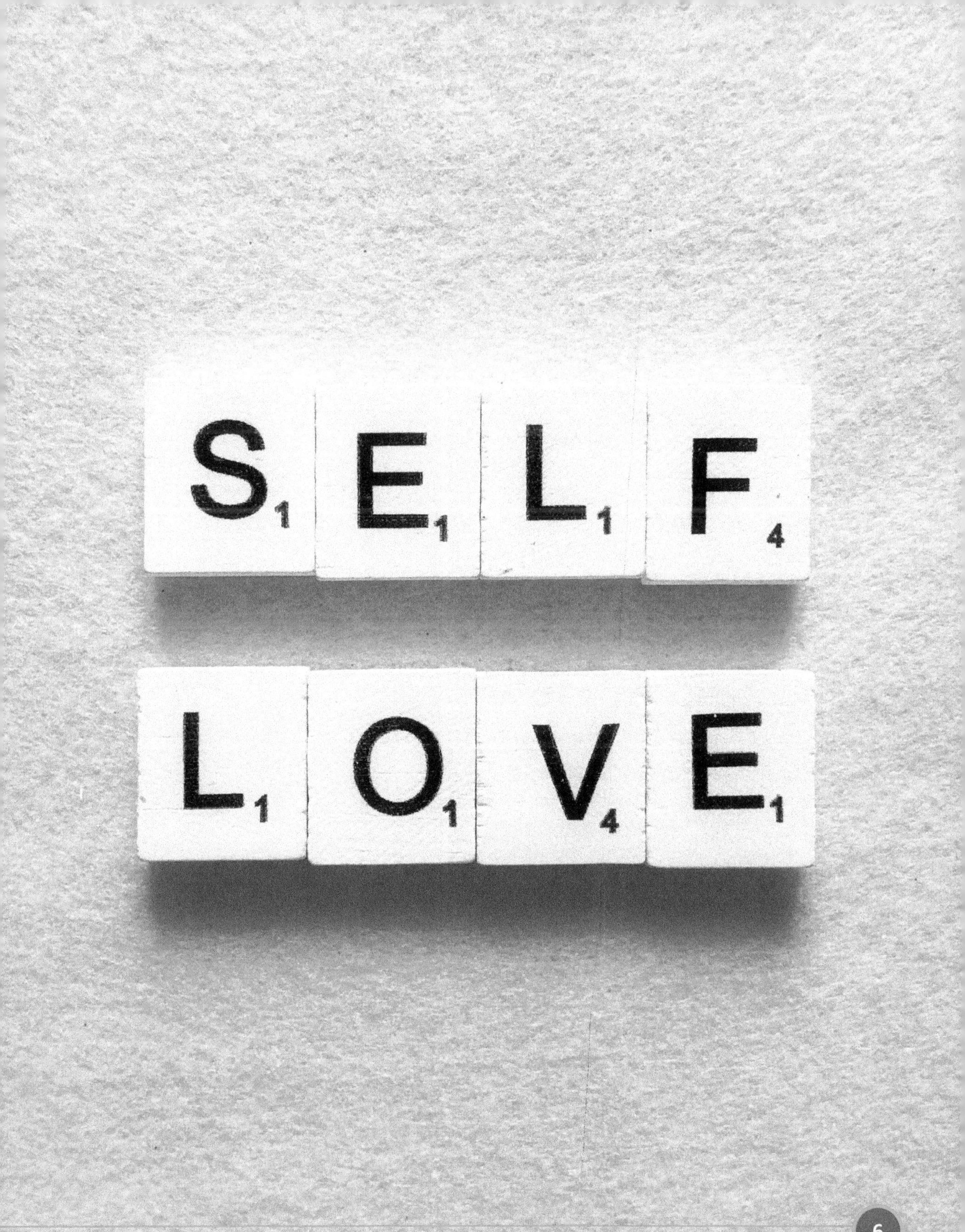
SELF
LOVE

Ingredients

-3 cups all-purpose flour
-3 large garlic cloves, minced
-1 tablespoon (or more, to taste) finely chopped fresh rosemary
-1 ¼ teaspoon kosher salt
-¾ teaspoon freshly ground black pepper
-½ teaspoon instant yeast
-1 ½ cups room temperature water
-2 tablespoons cornmeal

Directions

1. In a large bowl, combine flour, garlic, rosemary, salt, pepper, and yeast.
2. Using a wooden spoon, add water and mix until a wet sticky dough forms.
3. Cover the bowl tightly with plastic wrap and let it stand at room temperature for about 18-24 hours.
4. Lightly oil a 10-inch cast iron skillet and sprinkle with cornmeal.
5. Working on a lightly floured surface, shape the dough into a round.
6. Place dough into the prepared skillet. Cover with a dish towel and let stand at room temperature until dough has doubled in size and does not spring back when poked with a finger (about two hours).
7. Preheat the oven to 450°F.
8. Place in the oven and bake for 30-40 minutes, until golden brown.
9. Serve warm.

Emily Rose's No Knead Rosemary Bread

Adapted from damndelicious.net

Story

When I asked my mom how she chose my name, she responded with, "I don't know, it just sounded good together." And so that's how I got my name, Emily Rose.

When my Nonna answered the phone call from my parents at the hospital and heard the announcement that her first grandchild was born, she shouted "Ah! Amelia Rosa!" and my mom laughed and repeated, "No, it's *Emily Rose*."

"That's what I said," my Nonna replied.

And so I grew up with the most popular name of my birth year, and the year after that, and the year after that.

There were so many Emilys on my soccer team and in the halls at school that I developed the terrible habit of not responding to my name until I heard it for the third or fourth time. "Oh, me?"

"Yeah, I've been calling you!"

"Well, how was I supposed to know that?"

I am 50% Italian, Sicilian specifically, and 50% German/Welsh/Miscellaneous European. My mom isn't totally sure.

Growing up, we lived a few streets away from my Italian grandparents and I spent so much time there in my childhood that I smelled almost constantly of fried zucchini. Each Sunday was a spread: chicken cutlets, fresh bread, pastina (what we called Italian wedding soup), lasagna, meatballs, you name it.

But even in another language, I could tell what my grandfather was saying based on my grandmother's slumped shoulders and quick exit to the kitchen to get something or clean something or spend a minute without worrying about composure in front of "the family."

Two hours west, in rural Ohio, lived my mother's parents. Our meals were also incredible, yet wildly different than my other grandparents. Appetizers included Jell-O shaped like race cars, fruit pizza, chips, and a veggie tray with lots of ranch. We sat down in the dining room that overlooked the field and my grandpa would shout, "Look! A deer!" and steal food from our plates. Even when we *knew* the deer was our grandpa, we reacted the same each time—a wide eyed gasp, then a frown, then a laugh. There were mashed potatoes, buttered noodles, chicken and gravy, corn casserole, sweet rolls, and pop.

My older boy cousins at times were rough or mean to me, and I would tattle for relief. Once after dinner I tiptoed down the basement stairs and saw my uncle beating my cousin so badly he could hardly breathe through the tears. I walked back up the stairs feeling no longer like a child and sick to my stomach, as I looked at my mom who looked at her sisters who looked down at their plates.

In both houses we ate and talked and laughed.
In both homes we ignored and pretended and stood still through the storms.

When I was 25, I could no longer weather the storm in the same manner that I had for my whole life. I could no longer look down at my plate, tiptoe down stairs, or shove my feelings to the depth of my being. There was no room left to shove.

I wrote my dad a letter after years of emotional and psychological abuse, telling him that I could no longer live a life with him in it. It was the hardest thing I ever did, and my brain and body seemed to break in response to this hard stop. My nightmares got worse, the tension in my body increased, I clenched my jaw as if this constant state of activation and alertness could keep my brain and body safe.

In the five years since I wrote that letter, I have grown into a person. I slowly started to breathe. I slapped mortar on each brick one by one and built boundaries that were supportive of my dreams. I consumed the stories of others and found healing, then started slowly to tell my own.

Abuse and trauma can at times feel like a comparison game. "Well, they didn't _____, so it's not that bad." Or, "I always had a roof over my head and access to a good education." But under that roof was suffering, and suffering is not up for debate or comparison.

Because I chose to step away to heal, I lost many of the relationships I once had. I regretted not learning the recipes I enjoyed as a kid from my Nonna, and I felt too guilty for standing up for myself and "tearing apart the family" to go back and ask her to teach me.

In 2019, I learned how to make bread from a recipe I found while scrolling Pinterest. "No-Knead Rosemary Bread." It involved very few ingredients and looked downright delicious from the picture. When I mixed the dough, I felt a rush of emotions—nostalgia, joy, pride, and immense sadness. I used to help knead the dough for bread with my Nonna or squish the ingredients together for the meatballs, and my contact with these ingredients felt familiar and somehow lost in time.

The smell of garlic and rosemary filled my tiny kitchen, and the bread came out perfectly. I looked at it and shouted to no one, "I *made bread!*"

I love bread. Bread is my favorite food group, and yes, I count it as its own food group. But making this bread symbolized so many things, and in a way, I didn't even mean it to.

It felt like an accomplishment, that I could do something my ancestors did, and on my own. It felt like a door creaking ever so slightly open, that I could call my grandmother and share my success and maybe slowly repair an aching rift. It felt like the negative things got quieter, and the positive things got louder—breaking bread and laughing started to tip the scale toward forgiveness for the things gone wrong.

It also just felt damn good to cut into and lift that first slice to my nose and inhale as if I were taking my first breath all over again.

I am Emily Rose, and I can move through life with an understanding and open heart. I can move through the good and the bad and choose which I keep. I can make important decisions with impermanence and trust myself to make new decisions as people change, or don't change.

And you can, too.

You can make choices that you need to make, feel what you need to feel, shove when you have to, and unpack when it's safer.

You can live your life as you choose, and you can definitely make bread.

BIO

Emily Rose is a Nationally Certified School Psychologist, Registered Yoga Teacher, and author of the mental wellness blog, MissMagnoliaSays.com. She battled anxiety and depression in her youth due to what she describes as a delicious cocktail of nature and nurture. The cure for her was so simple and indescribably complex: human connection. Emily found healing in consuming the honest stories of others through a tall stack of memoirs that graced her nightstand, group and individual therapy, and connecting back with her body through yoga. Emily aims to bring this same sense of connection, plus a laugh or two, to her readers with each piece she writes.

Ingredients

-3 eggs
-1 cup oil
-2 cups sugar
-3 tablespoons vanilla
-2 cups grated zucchini
-3 cups flour
-1 tablespoon baking soda
-¼ teaspoon salt
-2 teaspoons cinnamon

Directions

1. In a large bowl, mix together the eggs, oil, sugar, and vanilla until mixed.
2. Add the zucchini and mix until incorporated.
3. Add in all remaining ingredients and stir with a wooden spoon until totally incorporated.
4. Bake at 350°F for 1 hour in a bundt pan or two loaf pans.

Emma's Zucchini Bread

Found

Found

When I was in middle school, I went through a *missed connections* phase. I would go online—Craigslist, virtual newspapers, online forums—and read the missed connections section. There was something about them that I found enthralling:

> *We were crossing Mass Ave at the same time. You had red hair and a matching red coat, I was hoping to get your phone number some time*

.

> *I complimented your golden retriever at the Commons and you told me a bad joke about bicycles. I'm wondering if we could meet up and exchange more bad jokes.*

> *You were in a blue Toyota at the red light on Main Street blasting the Trans Siberian Orchestra—we made eye contact but it turned green before I could say anything. Was hoping to connect with you again.*

It never mattered to me if they were mundane or absurd, if they were believable or a crazy creative writing exercise. To me, they were all real, for the simple reason that I wanted them to be. I lived in my head a lot, too, so I understood the feeling of catching a glimpse of a stranger and writing their story in your head, then deciding that the stranger you just dreamed up would be perfect for you. I loved thinking that sometimes the missed connections were found, that sometimes we can just imagine a stranger into being exactly who we want them to be if we just try hard enough. That we could imagine anything into being, if we tried hard enough.

Being chronically mentally ill is exhausting. Therapy, medication, nutrition counseling, practicing your skills, making appointments, keeping them. And there's burnout, too—for me, if I fell into the burnout and stopped being diligent about my medication, or stopped seeing my therapist every week, I would start to slide, to relapse into behaviors or coping mechanisms that were unhealthy and would lead to worse behaviors, increasingly declining mental health, things that jeopardized myself, my life.

For a long time, I felt angry about this. I felt it was unfair, that I shouldn't have to keep up with all of these things just to stay alive. I hated that I felt captive to my own brain, that it was so much effort to fight against these demons I didn't ask for, that I had to put in all this effort just to be above water when it seemed so easy for everyone else. As I said (often) to my therapist, *why is my own brain trying to kill me? How is that allowed?*

When I was lucky enough to finally have my head above water, I started to focus even more on this unfairness, feeling a growing sense of bitterness over how I didn't ask for any of this, didn't choose it, didn't want it. I thought back to my old love, the missed connections. There was a better version of myself out there, I knew it. There had to be. So I would write to the Better Me out there, hoping she'd read it.

> *You looked a lot like me, but your brain always made the right chemicals, and it never made you feel unsafe. Want to trade places?*
> *Same name, same face, but you never cry when you get dressed. Teach me your ways?*
> *It was like looking in a mirror, but you weren't afraid. What did you do differently?*

I wanted to believe I could find her. That I'd imagine her into being and fix all the things that I could only ever put a Band-Aid over. I'd play my favorite game for hours—*Who Would I Be If...?*—where I would envision how wonderful I could have been, if only I weren't so sick. It was the game that brought my mental health so low, and it was the game that brought it back up. Instead of avoiding the question entirely or giving into my brain's cruel thoughts, I faced the game head on. I wondered openly, not judgmentally—who *would* I be without these things? My struggles, as much as I have resented them at times, have made me who I am. Not because I identify *as* my illnesses, but because my journey with them has changed me. I've learned so much kindness, so much softness, so much strength. I have met people in treatment and in recovery who have changed my life forever, and who have shown me what it's like to have hope, to live fully, something I could never have imagined for myself before. The same skills and tools that I stubbornly resented learning are the skills that let me build true, authentic connections, something that I had never been able to do, and which changed my life for the best.

I won't pretend that I wake up every day and find joy in managing my mental health. Some days, it is still tiring. Some days, I still wish that it wasn't hard for me to do things that seem simple, that eating full servings was easy and answering texts didn't cause my heart to race. But I stopped looking for the better version of myself out there. I spent a long time searching, convinced something better was just around the corner. But I've learned there isn't—that the only version of myself is this one, whole and authentic and messy, enough just as I am.

You were waiting for me for a long time. I know I kept looking for someone else, but I'm ready now. Come meet me.

Ingredients

-¾ cups chocolate melts
-1 container fresh strawberries
-Cake pop sticks

Directions

1. Melt the chocolate in a microwave-safe bowl for 1-2 minutes.
2. Wash strawberries.
3. Push a cake pop stick into the stem of the strawberry and dip each strawberry into the chocolate.
4. Allow the excess chocolate to drip off.
5. Refrigerate for one hour and enjoy.

Gabby's
Chocolate Covered
Strawberries

Story

Reflecting across my glasses laying above my baggy eyes were the endless hours of streamed videos of the most accomplished individuals in our society. Video after video, with very little color, were men and women who were deemed successful giving speeches and accepting awards. I wanted to be them. I wanted to be in front of an audience, making a difference, accepting an award or giving a speech; however, I never believed that could be me, because I did not look like those people.

As a young child, I was ashamed and dishonored to be not only a person of color, but a LGBTQ+ woman of color. I felt inferior to the people on the screen because I did not see any-one who looked like me. Our society normalizes people of color and minorities as inferior to the white race. For so long, I wanted to be considered "normal" or "enough" and I couldn't understand why I felt so alone in feeling this way. However, as the present version of myself I realize the privilege white people have stems from the fact they never have to question their own identity the way people of color have to. Even within my own identity, I realize the privi-lege I have compared to other people's intersectionalities. The expectation to consistently rise above and battle through has felt like an additional weight of five extra people I have had to always carry on my back.

Balancing my mental health, academics, and my life in general has placed me in a position where it is difficult to handle all of them at the same time. If I focused on my mental health, I would set aside my academics and would have to catch up and do double the work to contin-ue climbing up the ladder of success. My achievements never feel sufficient because to me, they would never be enough to be successful. The term "Imposter Syndrome" derives from the feeling of being a fraud from all that you have accomplished. From my own experience, I can say this feeling has resonated with me since I entered this world.

Furthermore, intergenerational trauma has played a role in my upbringing. Although it is not my parents' fault for promoting the unhealthy habits that they were taught, I have to con-sistently unlearn and break the cycle. The Latinx community has raised older generations to believe that mental health is a myth and that having emotions makes us weak. We adapt to thrive in burnt out environments, but why live in a world where you can't be happy?

This past year and a half has been one hell of a ride—a bumpy one to say the least. I was able to take pit stops and do a lot of learning, unlearning, and most importantly (in my experience), healing. I learned that I had held on to so much pain not only caused by my own household or community, but specifically by society. I learned to be proud of my own identity. My caramel brown skin along with my accent from growing up in a Spanglish-speaking household was no longer something I should be ashamed of. I have learned that being LGBTQ+ was never meant to be something looked down on, but instead celebrated. The way I dress and show up in the world shouldn't have to fit in society's norm because, truthfully, society should be celebrating our differences in cultures, religions, sexualities, genders, styles, bodies, etc.

I hope to one day get rid of the bags under my eyes and replace them with wrinkles from smiling so hard they left marks. I wish younger me all of the love I have for myself now and I want her to know that everything will be okay. As I continue my journey in paving my own road, I will leave a few bumps along the way because without them, I wouldn't have recognized the perfections behind what I originally saw as imperfections within myself. I am proud of the journey I have started and I hope one day it will be streamed in front of the eyes of a girl like myself.

BIO

Gabby Alvarez (she/they) is a mental health, food justice, and social justice advocate. As a senior in high school, she strives to help those in her community rise above their struggles, whether this is through agricultural work at their job or at school as president of the Advocates for Social Justice Club. Gabby holds pride in being part of the LGBTQ+ community in addition to growing up in a Latinx household. Gabby hopes to pursue a career in social work and one day open her own non-profit organization.

Ingredients

-1 ¾ cup all-purpose flour
-2 ¼ teaspoon double-acting
  baking powder
-1 tablespoon sugar
-½ teaspoon salt
-¼ cup cold butter
-2 eggs
-⅓ cup cream
-1 cup brown sugar
-1 tablespoon cinnamon

Directions

1. Preheat the oven to 450°F.
2. Stir together in a large bowl: all-purpose flour, baking powder, sugar, and salt.
3. Cut into these ingredients, until it is the size of small peas, using two butter knives: ¼ cup cold butter.
4. Beat two eggs in a separate bowl.
5. Reserve two tablespoons of egg mixture. Add and beat in ⅓ cup cream to the remainder.
6. Make a well in the dry ingredients and pour the liquid into it.
7. Combine with a few swift strokes. Handle the dough as little as possible.
8. Place it on a lightly floured board.
9. Pat out until 1/2 inch thick. Sprinkle with a generous amount of brown sugar and cinnamon.
10. Roll the dough up, and then slice into about 12 rounds, placing onto a cookie or baking sheet.
11. Brush with reserved egg.
12. Bake for about 15 minutes.

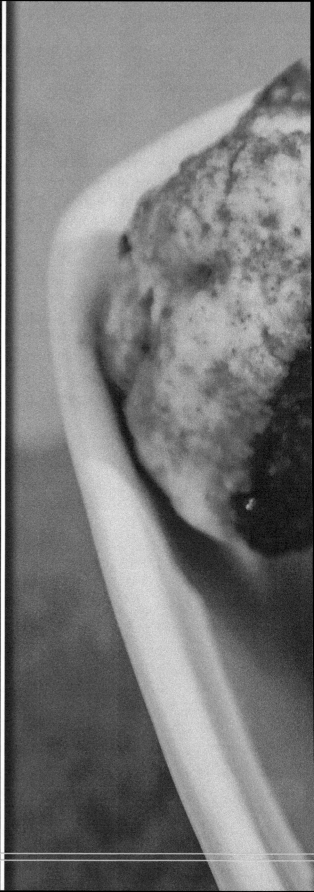

Alanna's Perfectly Imperfect Scones

Adapted from Joy of Cooking

Rewriting My Laws of Perfection

Rewriting My "Laws" of Perfectionism

It's 6:45 am on a Saturday morning, I'm on my second cup of coffee, have a load of laundry in, a two-mile run planned for later this morning before the rain starts (it's an unseasonably warm winter day in New England), along with lots of kid stuff, planning an upcoming vacation, and date night tonight with the husband to reconnect. Plus, there are thoughts—so many thoughts—swirling around my head as if I have 1000 different boxes open at once, and I'm already working. This is what it's like being a type-A, high-functioning, anxiety-driven perfectionist.

It's exhausting. Mentally and physically.

More than that, perfectionism is like a disease that spreads systemically through your life, sapping the joy. I'm always doing. It's never enough. And I'm judging, judging, judging myself at every turn. I'm not kind to myself and obsessively focus on lack: What's *not* there, what's *not* working, what *didn't* go right. It blocks me from seeing all the amazing things that are working, the beauty around me, the miracles that are happening right in front of me.

For years people have told me, with the best of intentions, to "lighten up," "relax," and "be kinder to myself." I tried. I did. And I tried with the vigor of the type-A, high-functioning, anxiety-driven person that I am. And I couldn't do any of those things with any consistency; I was never able to break free of the heavy burden of perfectionism.

Until last year. I was diagnosed with breast cancer. My life exploded with uncertainty and a forced loss of control—flinging me off the perfectionist train that I had been riding for decades. I saw how the years of harshing on myself, pushing myself, and beating myself up physically and emotionally played a part in my getting cancer. Maybe not directly, but indirectly feeding the engine of that never-enough train. Suddenly, my perfectionism wasn't just bad behavior, it was affecting my health. And if I truly wanted to get healthy—and I did—then I had to get to the heart of the matter, to the ground zero of where perfection breeds.

At the root of perfectionism are belief systems around how to behave, how to live, and how we explain why things happen. From these beliefs, we learn to judge ourselves. As children, we create these belief systems, influenced by our parents or caregivers. We didn't necessarily choose these beliefs, but we surrender to them unconsciously, and they become laws in our minds—our truth. We want to please our parents, we want to be liked, we want to do "good." This is where it starts.

For perfectionists, our laws go something like this:

"I must always be perfect."

"I'm not good enough."

"I should get everything right."

"If I don't do this perfectly, then everything will fall apart."

"If I don't do this perfectly, I will get hurt."

"I want people to like me."

"I'm not doing enough."

Perfectionists will tend to be the judge and jury of their lives, as Don Miguel Ruiz says in his book, *The Four Agreements*. The judge presides over every move we make, constantly deliberating as to whether or not we are living up to the laws we have created, never ruling in our favor—and using laws that don't even serve us. Not a very fair system. This is not justice.

Where does the anxiety come in? Well, anxiety is a perfectionist's best friend. It's like the gas in the perfectionist's car, the fuel that drives the fear of not being good enough and to keep on driving forward.

To begin to lift the burden of perfectionism, we have to first become aware of the laws that we are allowing to govern us. And then as the judge, we need to throw them out and rewrite them so that they serve us instead.

My rewritten perfectionist's laws:

"I am enough."

"I love and accept myself."

"My worth doesn't depend on my productivity."

"My worth doesn't depend on my work."

"I do not have to be perfect. I am human, and I am doing the best that I can."

"There is no reason to live up to impossible standards."

"Things won't fall apart if I don't single-handedly keep them going. And if they do, then they weren't meant to be."

Now, I've become vigilant in living by my new laws. I have to be. I recite them often, make them visible, write them down, repeat them in my head. I begin the day thinking of three things I love about myself and three things that I'm grateful for. I recall my new laws over and over; and occasionally, I'll default to the new laws over the old. When it happens, I notice it, relish it even, staying in the positive zone for a few seconds. A shift has begun. Now, these moments of new thinking happen more frequently, and eventually, the new laws will become stronger than the old.

Letting go, slowing down, and softening are also key. Perfectionists like control because it makes them feel safe. But it is a painful way to live. Now, I practice letting go by caring a little less about one thing coming up. Try to choose one thing. Maybe it's a work project or what someone thinks. Take a deep breath and tell yourself it's all good and everything will work out how it is supposed to work out—even if you don't fully believe it. Now, the judge will try to swoop in here and rule against the new caring-less laws. But just keep gently overruling, with self-compassion, telling yourself it's going to be okay.

Even when things don't work out as you had expected or wanted, allow the chips to fall where they may, and work to accept it, as it helps get you closer to where you need to be. For years, I have forced my expert control mojo to make things happen, many of which probably shouldn't have worked out that way—and wouldn't save for my sheer force of will. There have been jobs I have taken, plans made, vacations scheduled, friendships continued, all because I felt I "should." They weren't the right things for me in hindsight. There is more power in letting go and believing the universe will support you, because it will. Things will work out; maybe not the way we have planned, but possibly much, much better.

There *is* an upside to perfectionism: The sheer will and motivation creates a deep well of energy and drive for achievement. It has served me well. I was the editor-in-chief of a magazine at age 31, I have had a career that included being on all the major news networks, I've changed careers several times, I've written a book while working full time and raising two young children, and on and on. I've worked hard, *really* hard. But here's the thing that we perfectionists forget: you don't have to struggle to be successful. You don't. And joy isn't the result of struggle. Joy is the result of joy.

I'm a work in progress. As you can see from the Saturday morning routine, I sometimes slip back into old ways, especially when I feel overwhelmed. I also have to remind myself to be compassionate and forgiving when the shifts aren't happening as often or quickly as I would like. But when you begin to rewrite your laws of perfectionism, an entirely new world opens up. A world of possibility, of miracles, of joy, of lightness, of letting go of control, of flow, of kindness for yourself and others. Most importantly, it uncovers the real you underneath the perfectionism, and that is the best miracle of all.

BIO

Alanna Fincke, NBC-HWC, is a Board-Certified Health Coach and an expert in the science of resilience, teaching and training people in the top companies around the world as an SVP at meQuilibrium. She gives people the tools to transform and thrive both professionally and personally. A recent breast cancer survivor, Alanna has had to put her health and resilience to the test. She specializes in working with stressed "Type A's" as she is a recovering one herself—and moving them to what she calls, "Type H": healthy, happy, and healed.

Ingredients

-One full package of Oreo cookies (about 40)
-6 tablespoons butter
-16 ounces cream cheese
-½ cup granulated sugar
-1 teaspoon vanilla
-2 ½ cups heavy whipping cream
-1 ½ cups confectioners' sugar
-Hot fudge

Directions

1. Remove the filling from 24 Oreos and add the cookies to a food processor. Set the filling of cookies aside for a later step.
2. In a large bowl, add Oreo crumbs from the food processor with butter; stir to combine.
3. Pour the cookie mixture into the bottom of a 9x9-inch pan. Press dough into the bottom and up the sides to form a foundation for the cheesecake.
4. Place the pan in the refrigerator to chill.
5. In another large bowl, use a mixer to beat cream cheese until it is light and fluffy.
6. Add in sugar, vanilla, and the Oreo filling that was set aside to the bowl of cream cheese.
7. In a separate bowl, whip the heavy whipping cream with a hand mixer until it begins to thicken.
8. Add in confectioners' sugar and beat until stiff peaks form.
9. Fold two cups of whipped cream mixture and crushed Oreos (reserve ¼ cup for the garnish) into the cream cheese.
10. Pour mixture on top of the Oreo crust evenly.
11. Place in the refrigerator to chill for 4 hours or overnight.
12. Add Oreos with remaining whipped cream to the top of cheesecake with hot fudge.

Mekkailah's
No Bake
Oreo Cheesecake

Story

Content warning: Anxiety, Depression

Typing...*Backspace*...*Backspace*...*Typing*...*Backspace*

That's how it went for a while... I didn't know where to begin this story and I still don't really know what to say. I don't know what to do or how to do it. I don't know how to say no, and I don't know how to express myself.

Typing...*Backspace*...*Backspace*...*Typing*...*Backspace*

I've always been told that I didn't know anything. I was always called stupid and dumb, and that I could never do anything right. Every time I would make a mistake, I would get yelled at, and after constantly hearing those messages, I began to believe it. I believed that I was just someone who screwed things up and made them worse. So, it's not that I don't know how to start this off or even express myself, but I'm afraid of messing up. That little girl who was afraid then is still that girl today. Even at the age of seventeen, I've been told so many times that I could never do anything right that I began to believe that I was a mistake. From seeing my parents argue day and night, to seeing my mom wanting a divorce that never came, even then I felt like I did something wrong. Even if it had nothing to do with me, I felt like I could've done something to prevent those fights. Every little thing bothered me to the point where I thought I could've done something better and to be real, I still do. I found myself apologizing for almost everything, it became a habit. I'd overthink everything until I knew every outcome possible and I still do.

Typing...*Backspace*...Backspace*...*Typing*...*Backspace*

One thing I do know is that I've finally come to terms with the fact that I've gone through trauma. I think that a part of me just didn't want to accept it but in the end that is my reality. Whether it was seeing my parents get into arguments that were scary or seeing family members on their last few days on Earth. Whether it was being talked down on or just losing friends, I've come to realize that I have gone through trauma and for some reason, my mind has remembered all the bad and not the good. I had to grow up at a young age and in a way, I'm grateful. Despite all of it, it shaped me into who I am today.

Typing...*Backspace*...*Backspace*...*Typing*

For a while now I've also suffered from anxiety and depression. At first, I thought nothing of it and just figured it was just one of those days. I didn't want to accept the fact that

I couldn't do normal things like hang out with friends or family. I didn't want to accept that I didn't like the way I looked or talked. I didn't want to accept that sometimes I was just un-happy for no reason. As time went on, it just got worse and I was no longer sleeping or eating as much. I stayed up night after night, thinking I wasn't enough. I stayed up thinking that I shouldn't feel this way because others "had it worse." I never really spoke to anyone about it because I didn't want to "bother them with my problems." I didn't speak to my mom because things like this weren't normally spoken about in our household. I didn't know how to explain to her that I didn't want to be here anymore and how everyone would have it easier if I was gone. I never sought help because I wanted to prove to everyone that I could fix things, I could do things right for once. I just wanted to finally feel like I wasn't such a mess. Little by little, I have learned to live with these feelings and take each day as I go.

Typing...*Backspace*...*Backspace*...*Typing*

If I could ever speak to that little girl and change her mind, I'd tell her that she isn't a mistake. I'd tell her that she is human and simply just that. I'd tell her that she isn't stupid nor dumb and that I am proud of her. I'd tell these things to anyone because we all deserve to feel loved and needed. As humans, we tend to be our biggest critic and we never give ourselves enough credit for how far we've made it. No matter where you are in life, you deserve to be happy. You deserve to wake up and feel proud of yourself. You deserve to realize you made it... I've made it.

Typing...*Typing* ...*Backspace*...*Typing*

BIO

Mekkailah is a senior at Lynn Vocational High School and studies early education and care. Outside of her school life, Mekkailah takes pride in being a part of Skills USA and loves doing volunteer work. Currently, she works passionately alongside other youth and adults at the Food Project. During her free time, she loves to create and listen to music.

Ingredients

-1 20-ounce bag chocolate chips
-2 tablespoons milk (or your favorite non-dairy milk)
-1 pinch salt
-2 cups nut butter
-1 pinch cinnamon
-1 bag M&Ms

Directions

1. Melt the 20-ounce bag of chocolate chips over low heat. Add two tablespoons of milk (non-dairy milk works) or cream and a pinch of salt.
2. Once the chocolate is completely melted, pour half of the pot onto a baking sheet; spread evenly. Place the tray into the freezer to cool.
3. In a second pot, melt down two cups of the nut butter of your choosing with a sprinkle of cinnamon.
4. Once your nut butter has melted and your chocolate layer has frozen, remove your frozen layer of chocolate and add a layer of your melted nut butter over the top of the chocolate.
5.   Spread evenly and put your tray back into the freezer to set.
6. Once set, remove the tray again and add the remainder of your chocolate mixture onto the top. Spread evenly. Add as many rainbow M&Ms you would like over the top.
7. Put your tray back into the freezer to set and then you are ready to eat! Keep in the freezer or refrigerator.

Mallory's Peanut Butter Bark

Story

Demi-sexual? I guess that's the term they use to describe it. It's not about your gender or what you look like. It's the vibe, it's the connection, it's how you make me feel. The description sounds like the purest form of love because it's based on something more than the body you came in. That's not an attempt to take the moral high ground but simply the easiest way to explain this confusing attraction I have to an all-encompassing spectrum of people. I've sat in the company of all walks of life and felt an attraction not based in physicality but rather in the moments their personalities came through creating connection and shared experience. Writing it out sounds quite beautiful; feeling it is actually quite scary. In a society that is so hell-bent on telling you who and what to love it feels unnatural to feel anything outside of the ingrained heteronormative ideals. But I'm exhausted from stifling parts of myself for the comfort of others.

Beginning to understand one piece of my identity led to another revelation. Much of my life has been dictated by my desire to impress others; I've only ever wanted to be liked. I've never stopped to ask myself how I feel about the person I've become. Do I even like myself? Am I happy with the choices I've made or the way I present myself to the world? Honestly, I'm unsure if I've given myself a fair shot at this life. I've rarely let myself shine through in all of my wild and bright glory. It makes me sad. I'd never advise another soul to stifle their being, so I am finally attempting to embrace the many sides of me.

I'm attracted to people, not a gender. I have a mental illness, Major Depressive Disorder and Generalized Anxiety Disorder, to be exact, and I am unashamed to speak about it. I'm in love with experiences and emotions, not things. I'm most confident when a beat drops and my dance moves come alive. I have tattoos covering my wrists because I struggled with self-harm and wanted my wrists to be a work of art instead of a memory of pain. Hand me a lacrosse stick and you'll see me go from subdued to hype (okay, cocky) in record time. I hate small talk; tell me something real, something you feel, something with substance. I love doing nothing with the perfect company. I've never met a rock I didn't want to climb. I feel emotions with such depth that I cry at both the happy and sad parts of movies. If I spot a body of water you can guarantee I'll be beside it before you can blink your eyes. If you hand me chocolate don't expect to get any of it back. Sweats and funky socks are my true vibe. I still look at my hospital bracelet from my first inpatient stay ten years ago because I never want to forget the path I've taken to get to this point. Every song I like is "my jam." I'm most withholding with the people I most want to know me. If I've ever made you food I probably adore you. I'm afraid of getting close but crave closeness. I desperately want to come to a place of peace in my illness, even if that means peace in knowing we will continue to know each other forever.

I'm a work in progress, but I'm tired of hiding my illness, my sexuality, and my essence. I only have one chance at this life and I don't want it to be lived passively, quietly letting the days pass me by. My life was meant to be loud and proud. Cliché? Oh yes. But hey, it's my writing, my story, and my life. I'm going to own it.

And I hope more than anything, you also choose to own every quirk, every aspect, and every experience that makes you you. May we all live our lives unencumbered by the expectations of others, loud and proud.

BIO

Mallory is an unabashed mental health advocate who has spoken and written extensively on mental health and mental illness. She is now working full-time spreading joy, hope, calm, and comfort through her mental-health-focused business, Find Your/Self Boxes. If she ever has a spare moment she enjoys cooking and pretending she's a Food Network Star, hiking to find waterfalls with her friends, blasting an eclectic playlist of music while writing or dancing wildly (sorry neighbors), and cheering on the Baltimore Ravens on football Sundays.

COPING SKILLS AND TOOLS

When it comes to coping with stress, anxiety, or serious mental illness, everyone is unique and different in how they cope. There is not one skill or one tool that works for everyone, nor is there one skill or tool that works for every situation. In a lot of ways, learning what works for you can be like a puzzle, but the more tools you have, the more likely you are to have one that works!

You also don't have to ONLY use coping skills when you are in distress. In fact, it is better if you don't. The more you practice these skills, the easier they will be to access and utilize in a stressful moment.

Here are some suggestions of skills. Remember, there are many ways one can cope with stress and you never have to do so alone.

PLEASE NOTE: Coping skills are wonderful tools to use and practice when in stress, but if you are in crisis or in danger of hurting yourself or someone else, please call The National Suicide Prevention Lifeline at 1-800-273-8255 or text "HOME" to 741-741 for the Crisis Textline.

Coping Skills for the Moment	Coping Skill for Your Body
Write in a journal. Create something (bake!). Draw or paint. Move your body. Get some fresh air. Work on a project, puzzle, collage. Give back! Choose a random act of kindness. Make a phone call or write a letter to an old friend. Watch a show or movie, or listen to a podcast . Listen to music.	Regulate your breathing. Breathe in for 4, out for 2, repeatedly. Splash cold water on your face. Change the temperature in your body: take a hot shower, hold a frozen orange or towel. Take a brisk walk or exercise. Engage your muscles in progressive muscle relaxation. Light a candle to engage your sense of smell. Cry! Let it out! Drink a glass of water. Take a nap to reset. Take medication that is prescribed to you.

Coping Skills for Long-Term Impact	Write what helps you cope!
Recognizing your emotions. When you feel something, ask yourself what you are feeling and why (it is okay not to know why!) Validate your own emotions—you feel what you feel Practice kindness when talking to yourself Try detaching judgement from your thoughts, especially the negative ones! Don't believe everything you think! Work on doing what you want to do, rather than what you think you should do! Spend time with people who are good for your mental health, who you trust and who you feel good being around Go to therapy! Or find someone you can talk to! Take medication if prescribed and stay consistent in that Don't be afraid to ask for help	

Storytelling to Shatter Stigma

Author's Voice: The first time I ever told my story publicly, I practiced every day in a mirror for a month. Growing up as a theater kid, I was no stranger to the spotlight, but I couldn't imagine what it would be like to show up on a stage as me. Hiding behind a character and remembering lines was easy; speaking my truth in front of my mirror, let alone an audience, was inconceivably nerve-wracking. However, that never stopped me. Despite my legs shaking with nerves that first time, I felt so connected to a cause greater than myself, nothing else mattered. That cause being eradicating the stigma that surrounds mental health and mental illness, and that cause alone allowed me to persevere through all of the nerves and judgment I may have faced as a result. And seven years later, this still rings true! Although I don't always feel as nervous as I did the first night (I still get a bit nervous every time though), I continue to feel committed to sharing my story authentically, no matter where I am in the process. I feel honored that those who shared their stories here allowed me to do so, and I feel proud to be among such brave human beings who are willing to shatter the stigma that still exists when it comes to mental health. We have taken such wonderful steps toward deconstructing stigma when it comes to anxiety and depression, but we still have a long way to go in other areas of mental health. I am excited to be on the front lines of this fight along with those who share their stories here.

Ingredients

-2-3 very ripe bananas, peeled (about 1 1/4 to 1 1/2 cups, mashed)
-1/3 cup melted butter, unsalted or salted
-1 teaspoon baking soda
-1 Pinch salt
-3/4 cup sugar (1/2 cup if you would like it less sweet, 1 cup if more sweet)
-1 large egg, beaten
-1 ½ teaspoons vanilla extract
-1 ½ cups all-purpose flour
-Love

Directions

1. Preheat the oven to 350°F, and butter a 4x8-inch loaf pan.
2. In a mixing bowl, mash the ripe bananas with a fork until completely smooth. Stir the melted butter into the mashed bananas.
3. Mix in the baking soda and salt. Stir in the sugar, beaten egg, and vanilla extract. Mix in the flour.
4. Pour the batter into your prepared loaf pan.
5. Bake for 50 minutes to 1 hour at 350°F (175°C), or until a tester inserted into the center comes out clean.
6. Remove from the oven and let cool in the pan for a few minutes. Then remove the banana bread from the pan and let cool completely before serving. Slice and serve.

Abbey Wolf's Banana Bread

-IN LOVING MEMORY-

Story

Content warning: anxiety, depression, suicide

On May 3rd, 2006, Jon and Michelle Wolf welcomed their youngest daughter, Abigail "Abbey" Elizabeth Wolf, into the world and completed their family. Abbey joined their oldest daughter, Kayla, and middle son, David. Abbey was a shy toddler, but it didn't take her long until she was front and center, basking in the spotlight. Abbey didn't just enter a room, she would burst into a room... usually singing and dancing. Abbey didn't just light up a room, she created the room. She was authentic and she radiated pure love. Abbey was vibrant and kind with an infectious laugh. She was greatly admired, loved by all, and was everyone's friend.

Beyond her love of babies and animals, Abbey had so many interests—from sports and crafts to music and fashion and everything in between. Abbey was a fierce competitor, whether she was on the volleyball court or around the dining room table playing a game with the family. She didn't only craft, she was an entrepreneur—selling her homemade hand warmers, bracelets, and masks. Abbey loved Dan & Shay and Harry Styles. Grey's Anatomy was her favorite show. Abbey loved make-up and was an expert mascara applicator. You would never see Abbey without her signature white nail polish. She was a voracious reader, TikTok choreographer, and beach wave rider. She loved her family and she loved her best friend, Raleigh.

Abbey was compassionate, generous, and kind. She was always the first person to approach a new classmate or neighbor and make them feel welcomed. Abbey was bursting with talent, but was happiest when she was baking, earning her the nickname Martha Stewart. Sadly, Abbey also battled depression and anxiety and we tragically lost her to suicide on November 7th, 2020, at just 14-years old.

Abbey's Bakery was born out of her family's desire to honor Abbey's life and legacy, put their grief to work, and share the message that it's okay to not to be okay and it's okay to ask for help. Abbey's Bakery ultimately strives to prevent other families from experiencing this loss and pain.

Abbey's Bakery is dedicated to sharing Abbey's story, promoting mental health awareness & suicide prevention, and providing resources to those who may be suffering. They share Abbey's love of baking and her favorite Banana Bread recipe here in hopes that baking it brings joy and happiness and creates an environment that fosters mental health conversation. Abbey's Bakery strives to normalize mental health conversations and end the stigma against mental illness and suicide.

Abbey's Bakery regularly participates in events where they sell their mason jar baking mixes, accept donations, and share resources. All proceeds benefit mental health and suicide prevention initiatives. You can learn about upcoming events, see how to donate, and of course find resources at abbeysbakery.com. You can also find them on Facebook & Instagram @abbeysbakerycharity.

The world is a better place for having had Abbey in it. We love and miss you every minute of every day. Be Sweet, Sing Loud, Dance Often, and Bake with Love.

Ingredients

-1 box red velvet cake mix and ingredients listed on the box
-1 stick unsalted butter, softened
-1 8-ounce cream cheese brick, softened
-1 teaspoon vanilla extract
-¼ teaspoon salt
-4 cups powdered sugar
-6 mason jars
-Sprinkles

Directions

1. Preheat the oven to 350°F.
2. Follow instructions on the red velvet cake mix box and bake.
3. Let the cake cool.
4. In a bowl with a stand mixer, combine butter and cream cheese and beat until creamy or without lumps.
5. Add vanilla extract and salt, stir to combine.
6. Gradually add each cup of powdered sugar until completely combined.
7. Wash a mason jar and with the lid, cut out three layers of red velvet cake.
8. Layer the red velvet cake with cream cheese frosting, alternating a layer of cake, a layer of frosting in the jar. Repeat for all six jars.
9. Add red sprinkles for effect.
10. Keep refrigerated and enjoy!

Dev's Red Velvet Cake-in-a-Jar

Story

Five Crucial Moments

1st crucial moment: I grew up with love. Lots of love from my family, lots of love from my friends. Life was really quite easy for me and I am blessed for the things I have had in my life that made my childhood the best it could be. I was getting B's and C's in school, playing excessive amounts of video games, hanging out with my three best friends whenever I could. I'd come home to a loving family consisting of my mother, father, and sister for a while, until my parents divorced and my sister went to college. My parents are still good friends. I want to point out that you can clearly see I had an easy-going childhood; so you may be wondering, what happened to me?

2nd crucial moment: I smoked marijuana recreationally in high school. To put it logistically, I was someone who logged every time I smoked because both my mom and I knew that I was taking a risk—my family has an addiction history. I used marijuana 94 times and binge drank alcohol only around a dozen times between the ages of 16-18. Marijuana was extremely euphoric until it eventually turned to paranoia… something *much* worse than I could have ever imagined.

3rd crucial moment: In my astronomy class during my senior year of high school, I suddenly felt extremely paranoid. Strange.

I began to think: *It couldn't have been from marijuana since that day I hadn't smoked. So, I knew I wasn't high. It couldn't have been from lack of sleep because my sleep schedule was good and consistent.*

I didn't know it yet, but this was the onset of psychosis.

I felt like all of my peers in class were staring at me. I left school at the end of that class. I drove home and curled up in the fetal position on my couch; my entire world felt like it was collapsing in on me.

See, marijuana was what exacerbated my illness. It is the reason that I became what is known as psychotic or having psychosis. My entire life was flipped upside down for six months; I was inexplicably paranoid and terrified. In order to explain this to someone who hasn't had psychosis, I ask you to imagine having a microphone on a maximized volume level magnify every thought that goes through your head for six months. To make it even more unbearable, imagine that your mind's way of thinking is chaotic and disorganized; my memories were mixed with delusions. I did not have any self-awareness—I didn't know what was happening to me. I had thoughts I couldn't keep to myself, such as my spiritual delusion that I was indeed Jesus Christ.

My symptoms when I was psychotic were: thought-broadcasting, disorganized thinking, delusions, paranoia, and panic attacks. I admitted myself to a hospital for one week... that was eventful, to say the least. For six months, I struggled through (what I imagine will be) the worst period of my entire life. My brain was bruised. I needed to heal, I needed to recover, and I needed it to happen NOW and FAST because this was unbearable. Every day I would go on walks with my mom and ask her when I was going to get better and when the medicine would kick in. My life for these six months consisted of as many distractions as possible. Until during month four, when things started to click...

4th Crucial moment: For 15 seconds at a time, I began to feel clarity and like the medicine I was taking was working. Colors were more vibrant, the disorganized thinking turned organized again. But then it slowly faded away. I never lost hope, though, and I found optimism, intro-spection, and improvement through this time; I felt like this optimism was radiating from my aura.

At this point I was starting to think about the idea of briefly seeing two of my best friends in person. They were so worried about me; so, we followed through with meeting up. When they first saw me, they had no idea what to expect. The atmosphere was a bit hectic, there was little eye contact from me. The three of us sat on the couch... the same couch I was in a fetal position on just four months earlier.

I told them, "I had been isolating myself from seeing anyone other than my mom." They said, "As long as you're better, man, we are here for you." We cried together—tears of relief. My brain was beginning to see the light at the end of the longest tunnel I had ever been trapped in. It was really a miraculous happening.

Around this same time, after leaving my psychiatrist's office one day, my father coincidentally noticed a ballroom dance studio next door. My dad suggested I try out a few lessons, another distraction. This suggestion not only helped speed up my healing process, but ballroom danc-ing also proved to be my first passion.

My brain began to heal very, very gradually! Finally, IT GOT BETTER.
I wanted to give my support team all the credit; they told me I did most of the work, though, and that I should be very proud of myself. And I still am.

Now, fast forward three years, I had a second psychotic break on my 21st birthday, where I admitted myself to another hospital. It was the best birthday gift I could have given myself;

I asked for help, and I received care. And this psychotic break only lasted one month! At this point, I was diagnosed with schizophrenia. But this didn't phase me.

5th crucial moment: The number of positives that have come out of this are miraculous, to say the least, and there have been so many moments since I have been proud of.

I've had no psychotic symptoms for the past four years, which means I no longer need to cope with anything other than regular life. I've accumulated a dense "Tool Kit" over the years, with over thirty self-made tools in order to cope with both my past psychotic symptoms and present, everyday social experiences. I still go over my tools with my family therapist, because I believe it can only help.

I am very self-sufficient now in finding activities to entertain myself, such as playing piano, singing, talking with friends, caring for animals, working at my new job, and the list keeps growing. Rightly so, I proudly wear my schizophrenia like a badge of honor. I defeat stigma by just living as Dev.

I have won over a dozen 1st place ballroom dance ribbons in competitions and danced in two blockbuster films next to Jennifer Lawrence and Chris Pine.

I graduated with Magna Cum Laude honors from a university where I majored in performing arts and minored in creative writing. I passed my CPS exam, and every day through my job, I get to help people between the ages of 14-30 find hope in their lives.

And most of all, I can finally say that I am 100% recovered. I have never felt as secure and resilient as I do today, and I have permanently refrained from drinking and drugs.

I have a life now that is even better than *before* I had psychosis. I have become more empathetic, friendly, independent, healthy, successful, confident, socially adept, articulate, and I have uncovered talents I never knew I had. Also, through sharing my story, I've become an aspiring public speaker with a passion to collaborate; I have evolved.

I want to thank my specialists, therapists, doctors, family, and all of my best friends for their tremendously vital support. I also want to thank myself.

I am Dev. I am hope. I am schizophrenia strong.

BIO

A passionate 25-year-old, Dev is a graduate of Roger Williams University with Magna Cum Laude honors. He received his bachelor's degree in the performing arts with a minor in creative writing. He genuinely values betterment, optimism, and honesty. He loves to develop his many talents which include, but are not limited to: acting, singing, dancing, piano, public speaking, and weight-lifting. When not improving his talents, he thoroughly enjoys going out socializing, listening to electronic dance music, video gaming, spending time with his close friends, being with his pet cats, and going on adventures. Dev works to crush the world's stigma around mental illness with his triumphant mental health story.

Ingredients

-1 box angel food cake mix
-1 ⅓ cups water
-1 container cool whip
-1 container strawberries

Directions

1. Follow instructions on the angel food cake mix box.
2. Bake at 350°F for 40 minutes.
3. Let cool.
4. Cut in half when cooled.
5. Add two cups of cool whip to each side.
6. Wash and cut strawberries.
7. Decorate with strawberries.
8. Enjoy!

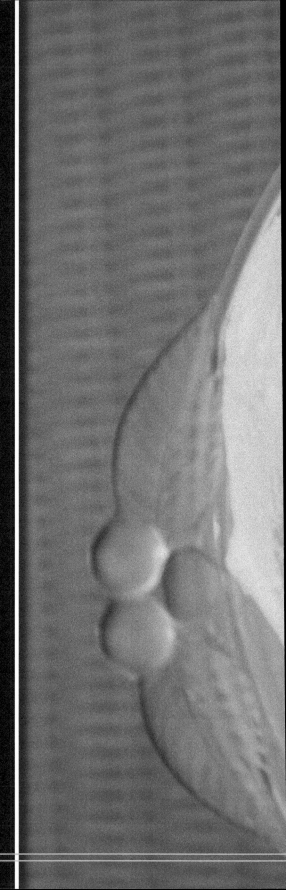

Laura's Angel Food Birthday Cake

Story

Being the youngest in my family has undoubtedly shaped me as a person. Having two older siblings struggle with their mental health even before I came along set the stage for a very understanding and open family dialogue about mental health. I feel lucky in this capacity because when I started to struggle, I didn't have to suffer in silence.

As I write this now, I feel like I am in the acceptance stage of my mental health story. Earlier this year, I went on medication for my anxiety, which was a big step. I also know that where I am with my eating disorder is a place of recovery, and I am proud of that.

My struggles with my body really began in high school. Growing up in an affluent town, I felt like appearance was at the center of every conversation and it was certainly on my mind. I heard people talk about and berate their bodies and I would think, "If you are fat, then what am I?"

These insecurities continued to manifest when I went off to college. I had this overwhelming amount of guilt around food all the time. I felt guilty when I was eating, I would feel guilty when I wasn't exercising and I was looking for someone to take the guilt away because I could not do that for myself. This coincided with my own idea that I was going to find the love of my life within the first few weeks of college. And when I did find someone I liked at the beginning of school, I was crushed to find out the feelings were not mutual.

I felt like I was not enough for anyone. My insecurities grew and when I went home the following summer, I developed a binge eating disorder. I associated food with guilt. Because I really only binged and never did the "diet part" I felt like a failure of person and of an eating disorder. I lost total control and this impacted my life negatively in every way.

The following fall during my sophomore year, I was at rock bottom. Two of my best friends transferred out of my school and both of my grandmas had passed away within a month of each other, among other family stress. I was so tired of feeling this way.

There was not one turning point for me, rather there were several things that helped me move from being depressed, guilty, and hopeless to grounded and empowered. One of which was falling head over heels for someone who actually saw my value, and while we are no longer dating, finding love for myself through love from another was truly healing. I also transferred schools and the summer before transferring, I started working at a restaurant with my friends. Surrounding myself with people that I loved and loved me helped me move forward in feeling accepted. While these things did not solve all of the problems, it did help me take steps toward recovery. And even though my weight had fluctuated when transferring and then traveling, I was just so happy, it didn't matter. I began to love who I was and that was at the forefront of my life.

Today, I work at a non-profit that is centered around female empowerment. While I have many different responsibilities at work, one of the most rewarding parts of my job is teaching a Body Positive curriculum to the teen girls I work with. So many of the messages I get to teach through this curriculum are things I wish I knew years ago... like, it is okay to trust your body. I also have come to a place of including mental health in my own definition of health, and that there is so much more to a healthy life than the way you look. I have reframed my brain to recognize that mental health comes first and that I don't have to feel guilty for eating or breathing, for that matter. I am, in fact, enough, simply because I exist.

Ingredients

-1 cup flour
-½ teaspoon baking soda
-⅛ cup vegetable oil
-½ cup natural peanut butter*
-½ cup apple sauce
-½ cup pumpkin puree**
-1 egg
-½ cup plain Greek yogurt

*do not use a peanut butter with xylitol, it is dangerous for dogs
**pure pumpkin, not canned pumpkin pie mix

Directions

1. Preheat the oven to 350°F.
2. In a large bowl, combine flour and baking soda.
3. In a separate bowl, mix ¼ cup peanut butter, apple sauce, vegetable oil, and pumpkin puree.
4. Once mixed, add in egg and mix until combined.
5. Combine wet and dry ingredients and stir until combined.
6. Grease an 8-inch round pan and pour in mixture.
7. Bake for 25-30 minutes and let cool.
8. Mix Greek yogurt and 1/4 cup peanut butter until well combined.
9. Add frosting to cooled cake and store in the refrigerator.

Jenna's Dog Birthday Cake

Humans Can Eat It Too

Emotional Support Animals: This is Not Fake

Content Warning: Mention of trauma, anxiety, depression

Emotional Support Animals
This is Not Fake

The first time I held Otis in my arms, he was handed to me by two strangers taking him out of a crate in a van that had just had a long trip to Connecticut from Tennessee. He was so scared. I was too. I cried as they put his thirteen-pound, shaking little body in my arms and kissed the top of his head. "It'll be okay," I whispered to him. I needed to hear those words, too.

Otis is my emotional support animal (ESA). This is not a fake title. Yes, there are many websites you can use to get a letter from a real doctor that says you need an animal for emotional support. No, I did not do this. My psychiatrist wrote the letter. His title as an ESA is not fake and is actually recognized by the Fair Housing Act and a few other laws. He's like a holistic prescription, if you will.

There are a lot of critics on the subject of ESAs. I get it. It's very easy to Google the phrase and find 100 websites willing to offer you a letter saying that you clearly need this animal for the low price of $200! But I didn't adopt Otis as some form of a scam, as a way to trick my landlord, or as a way to get my dog to travel for free; I got Otis because I need him.

Okay, we can go back to the word need. Technically, I don't need him, but he helps. I was diagnosed with General Anxiety Disorder and Major Depressive Disorder years ago, and since then, the symptoms of both have only increased.

In the years between my diagnosis and the adoption of Otis, too much happened for me to deal with alone. My best friend died by suicide, I lost both of my grandparents, I found out I'd never met my real father, I was sexually assaulted, and my uncle was murdered. And that's just the big stuff. Not even the everyday little triggers that we all deal with.

Too much happened for even my medications, my therapist, my psychiatrist, and group therapy to help me cope sometimes.

So in came the idea of an ESA. I'd grown up with dogs my entire life and noticed that I was just happier around them. They were a distraction, something to focus my mind on. So for two weeks I browsed adoption websites, and found my ESA—Otis.

I'm not going to pretend I know psychologically why Otis has helped me so much. Why, in the time since I've gotten him, I've felt better when I wake up. Like I can actually get out of bed and maybe even make it through the day. What I do know is this—he needs me, and I need him.

Otis is the first animal I've ever met that has really made me wonder—who rescued who?

<u>Bio</u>
Jenna Malley is a young professional currently living and working in the Greater Boston Area. Originally from New Jersey, Jenna earned both her master's and bachelor's degrees in chemistry at Northeastern University; this is also where she also met her husband! Jenna is passionate about mental health advocacy and dog rescue. She founded her own 501(c)(3) non-profit, The AMAZING Campaign, in memory of her best friend that lost her life to suicide. Though she has a crabby rescue dog of her own, she actively fosters dogs and volunteers in any way that she can to assist the rescue group Last Hope K9.

Ingredients

-1 box Devil's Food cake mix and associated ingredients (egg, oil, water)
-4 cups milk
-2 boxes chocolate pudding
-2 cups heavy whipping cream
-½ cup mini chocolate chips for topping

Directions

1. Prepare Devil's Food cake according to package instructions in a 9x13-inch baking dish
   and bake until a toothpick inserted in the
   center comes out clean.
2. While the cake is baking, prepare the two
   boxes of chocolate pudding with the four
   cups of milk. Place in the fridge until ready to
   use.
3. When the cake has cooled, poke holes (with
   the handle of a wooden spoon or something
   similar in size) all over the cake, poking all the
   way down to the pan.
4. Pour the pudding mixture over the cake, using the back of a spoon to spread the pudding
   over the top, making sure it gets down into
   the holes. Place the cake in the refrigerator to
   cool.
5. Once cooled, spread prepared whipping
   cream over the top of pudding, sprinkle with
   chocolate chips as desired.
6. Refrigerate until ready to serve and keep in
   the fridge to store.

George's Chocolate Pudding Cake

Story

My parents divorced when I was very young. I was born five years apart from my two older brothers, so they were old enough to understand what was going on, while for me, this was more confusing. For the next eighteen years, my parents would swap custody of us every week. One week living with my mom, the next week I was living with my dad. School vacations and holidays would be swapped too: "Thanksgiving at dad's and your mom can have Christmas." That's how my schedule went for eighteen years of my life. It wasn't perfect and we all went through difficult transitions and struggles, but in hindsight (compared to my friend's divorced parents), it was the most stable any divorced family could be. Both of my parents remarried people that love and care for them.

Fast forward to 2013, I graduated high school and joined the National Guard on a six-year contract. Everything was going as planned. I joined my new unit, met my future wife, and started school. Things were pretty good. Then as time went on, I didn't have the energy to keep up with it all. It was an exhausting schedule with standards that I couldn't live up to. It became overwhelming and I just couldn't do it. I began to feel empty inside, despite having the support of my partner. She advocated that I needed to tell someone what was going on, but this wasn't easy for me. I was able to call my Squad Leader and he was able to get me the help I needed right away. But I would not have asked for help if it was not for my wife advocating for my mental health. I was entitled to the help I needed but I was too afraid to ask for it, thinking that it would make things worse. With my wife's advocacy, the National Guard connected me to mental health resources I needed to make sense of what I was feeling. This part of my life taught me how important it is to speak up about mental health and the importance of the people who make the effort to support it. It was those people who helped me get up in the morning and keep moving forward.

Ingredients

-5 eggs
-1 ¼ cups vegetable oil
-1 can solid-pack pumpkin
-2 cups flour
-2 cups sugar
-2 packages vanilla pudding mix
-1 teaspoon baking soda
-1 teaspoon ground cinnamon
-½ teaspoon salt

Directions

1. Preheat the oven to 325°F
2. In a small mixing bowl, begin the recipe by beating eggs.
3. Next, add oil and pumpkin; beat until smooth.
4. Combine remaining ingredients to gradually create a pumpkin batter.
5. Pour batter into five small, greased loaf pans.
6. Bake at 325°F for 50-55 minutes.
7. Let cool on a wire rack and enjoy.

Lindsay's Pumpkin Bread

Story

Content warning: Mentions of eating disorder behaviors, self harm, anxiety, depression

My journey with mental illness and mental health struggles began after the worst year of my life. Within a year (the end of eighth grade to the end of my freshman year), my parents separated, which resulted in my dad moving out; my mom was diagnosed with breast cancer; we had to put our dog down; and I lost my very best friend unexpectedly. No, she did not pass away or move, but she disappeared from my life, which, in a way, is more painful. So much anxiety, fear, and loss for a 14-or-15-year-old who was also attending a brand new school and knew only one person going in. After my year from hell, I began my sophomore year and prayed it would be a better year. In a sense, it was; my mom was healthy and my dad was happy. We had a new dog, who did not replace my first dog but helped fill part of a hole in my heart. On the surface, I was great. But underneath, I felt as if I was drowning. People saw me as "the sad girl," and it wasn't until my school nurse noticed me that I began to come to terms with everything. My coping mechanism at the time was to eat my feelings until they were gone. If I shoved everything far enough down, it would go away, right? Wrong. Not only did it stay, but it bubbled up when I least expected it, which was painful all over again. After many times of talking to my school nurse, she decided to call my mom and recommend that I start therapy. After that, things happened so fast. I had my first therapy appointment and then had one every week for about a year. But I never talked about anything real that was bothering me because I wasn't comfortable. It wasn't until months later that I found someone I really liked and realized that my first therapist just wasn't the right fit for me. During the winter of my junior year, I talked to my doctor, and we realized that therapy alone wasn't enough for me. I went on antidepressants and have been on them ever since. The combination of medication and therapy worked for me. I continued seeing my new therapist until the second half of my senior year. While figuring out what treatments worked for me, I also became very involved in my church and my faith. It became a safe space for me and a place where I could leave every-thing behind and simply be in the moment. Having something outside of school to turn to and feel like I belonged was key for me and my mental health.

At the beginning of March 2020, we were sent home from school due the global pandemic and we did not return. We continued classes online in a very unstructured fashion. If this wasn't hard enough, I thought I had lost someone I was very attached to. I began working with the newly hired adjustment counselor at my high school to manage my anxiety and depres-sion. I was grieving the loss of this important person and at the end of my senior year of high school, I went through a period of self-harm and at one point was evaluated by a mobile crisis service. They came to my house and did a safety and psychiatric evaluation. They determined that I was not a risk to myself and therefore did not need to be placed in an inpatient facility. I was relieved and disappointed at the same time. Part of me wanted to go to an inpatient facility because I thought it would fix everything. But the other part of me did not want to put my parents through that. Eventually, I began to feel better each day and exercise became a very important part of my life at this time. At first, exercise was structured and made me feel good. At a certain point though, it became complicated for me. I struggled with disordered eating and began to partake in unhealthy ways of making me feel better about my food choices. To this day, I struggle with my relationship with food, but it is becoming easier.

Last year, I began my freshman year at Simmons University in my childhood bedroom. We had hoped to be on campus for the spring semester but that did not happen. Classes on Zoom for a whole year while adjusting to a new workload was incredibly challenging and stressful. I reached out to the counseling center and got paired with one of the MSW interns. I worked with her through the whole year to navigate leaving high school behind and not being able to move to school. I went through so many ups and downs and having someone to talk to was very helpful. While I had my struggles and went through even more losses, I was determined to keep my grades up and do well in school. I made Dean's List both semesters of freshman year. Towards the end of my first semester, I began a new job at the same daycare I attended when I was little. This job allowed me to work with kids and it quickly became my happy place. I started working mostly with the infants and absolutely loved—and still love—my job. I found a place where I feel appreciated and wanted, and that is the greatest feeling in the world to me. This job was a breath of fresh air compared to my previous one, which had a terrible work environment.

I cannot wait to move to campus for my sophomore year of college and begin a brand-new chapter in my life. I am in school for Social Work and am part of the 4+1 MSW program at Simmons. Once I finish school, I want to work in the mental health field, helping teenagers and young adults. While I have faced countless hard times over the years and will likely face countless more, I am proud of how strong I have become and the person I have grown into! I am thankful for everything I went through because it helped me figure out what I want to do with my life and what purpose I want to serve. I am so grateful for my family and friends, who have supported and loved me through everything. I cannot wait for all of the amazing things in the years to come!
To those reading this, please know your worth and how much you have to offer in this world. So many people love and appreciate you and want you in this world. Even when times get hard, know your strength and please never give up! I believe in you and hope you believe in yourself!

BIO

Lindsay Albright is a college student studying Social Work at Simmons University. She is currently in a 4+1 MSW program. Outside of the classroom, she is getting involved in clubs and activities, including Jumpstart as an AmeriCorps member. Before moving to Boston for school, she spent her days working at The Goddard School with infants and toddlers. Lindsay is very passionate about issues surrounding mental health and wants to work in an inpatient facility as a Social Worker once she has finished school and received her Master's of Social Work. Her hobbies include working out, exploring the city with friends, and working with little kids!

Ingredients

-1 cup old fashioned oats
-½ cup ground flax meal
-½ cup chocolate chips
-½ cup peanut butter
-⅓ cup honey
-1 teaspoon vanilla

Directions

1. Mix oats, flax meal, and chocolate chips into a medium bowl.
2. In a large bowl mix peanut butter, honey, and vanilla.
3. Pour dry ingredients into the wet ingredients and mix together.
4. Put in refrigerator for 20 minutes (so that it is easier to form mixture into balls)
5. Roll into bite size balls (about 1 inch) and put them on a cookie sheet or plate and they are ready to eat!

Zita's
No Bake
Energy Bites

Story

Have you ever been paralyzed with fear? I have actually lived most of my life terrified. When I tell you what I am scared of, you may think it is silly—but to me it couldn't be more real. I was diagnosed with OCD when I was in fifth grade. OCD stands for Obsessive Compulsive Disorder. It is when your brain misfires and puts a fearful thought in a cycle where it tells you to do a behavior to make everything fine—but then you have to do it again and again.

OCD is a very bossy disorder. It installed fear in me so I would do what it wanted. "Wash your hands, Zita." I would get some relief, but then OCD would say, "Now wash them again, or you will get sick and die." Again. Again. Again. This happened until there was no skin left on my hands to wash. "If you bump or touch one of your friends, Zita, she will die. Avoid your friends at all costs; it will keep them safe." "Apologize, Zita. Everything you do is wrong, and if you don't say you're sorry, everyone will hate you." These are just a few lies that OCD told me. Imagine living with that voice in your head, and now imagine me as a little girl trying to conform to this. Did I want to die? No—so I washed my hands. Did I want my friends to die? No—so I stayed away from them. Did I want to get in people's way, mess things up? No—so I apologized for every move I made.

I was in Cognitive Behavioral Therapy (CBT) for five years. Throughout this therapy, I learned how to train my brain to stop the repetitive behaviors. For example, one of the ways that helped me with my compulsive hand washing was using little chips. Each morning I would get twenty chips; each time I washed my hands I would have to take a chip away. I had to make it with only 20 hand washes for about an hour, this was the hour before I got on the bus. This may seem like an easy task for some people, but I had to plan my whole morning around when I was going to wash my hands. Then each week I would have less chips—which meant less hand washes. Slowly, I didn't need to wash my hands so much. This did not happen overnight, but through years of work.

I still have hard days. I may not need to wash my hands all the time, but my brain sometimes shuts down. I get so overwhelmed that I can't function. Last lacrosse season, I had to be pulled out of the goal in lacrosse because I shut down. Last week, after school, I couldn't drive my car because OCD was driving me. But I have overcome a lot, and I have worked so hard to do so. But there will still be days of darkness and days of light.

Everyone has been dealt a hand of cards, and they are not always fair. But you can't let that define you. You are more than your burdens. I know I am more than Zita Who Has OCD. I am Zita, who happens to have OCD, but it doesn't define me. We all have a secret, and if you don't know what you're good at or what makes you special—ask your friends! We are all strong, special, and gifted in our own way. So stand up and don't let problems define you.

This is an excerpt from a speech I gave in front of the entire student body when I was a senior in high school. I thought that once I brought light to the secret I had held onto for years, the OCD and anxiety was in the past. I had called it by name, so therefore I thought it had no more power. Unfortunately, as I would learn to this very day—it does not just disappear.

For me, fighting against anxiety and OCD is like playing a sport. I had the privilege of playing lacrosse from middle school to the collegiate level, and combating anxiety is similar to preparing for practice and games. Sometimes, you show up and it's sunny and it's ideal playing weather. Other times you show up and it's raining, the ball is less visible and you are drenched. But either way—to continue to get better at lacrosse—you have to show up. Sometimes you can predict how the other team will act and prepare for it, other times you are blindsided by how they run their plays. I have lived with anxiety and OCD for over twenty years. Some days, when I wake up, it's "raining" and I'm blindsided, being paralyzed by panic. Those are the days that are extra tiring because I still need to show up and use the skills I have practiced and learned in therapy to keep moving forward during the day. However, those bad days serve a purpose—they make the good ones that much better. So when the good days come (and they always do), the sun shines that much brighter and the anxiety takes a backseat.

Up until recently, I forgot about my favorite part of lacrosse: it is a team sport. No matter the circumstance (rain or shine) or team you were up against—you were not alone. You had a group of people who were right there alongside you, fighting with you, pushing you to keep getting better, supporting you when you were tired and exhausted, and motivating you to put one foot in front of the other. And you did, because you knew no matter what, they had your back. Over this past year, I have realized that when I go up against the really hard days, I am not alone. I have a team—they might not be carrying lacrosse sticks, but my chosen family is in my corner—and they won't let me go in it alone, they have my back. They continue to remind me that the bad days do not last forever, and there are always great days ahead (no matter how it might feel in a singular moment—it is just that: a moment). They meet me where I am and walk alongside me, reminding me to put one foot in front of the other—because one step forward (even just one) is still progress.

So, I learned it's okay to be afraid and anxious—it gives me the opportunity to be brave and strong. The anxiety will come and go like waves—I just have to continue to show up no matter what, because when it gets tiring and it feels too overwhelming, all I need to do is look to my left and my right and see my team cheering me on, taking each step forward with me. So no matter the situation (rain, snow, or shine), I know I will never walk it alone.

Ingredients

- -3 ½ cups apples
- -2 cups sugar
- -3 cups flour
- -1 teaspoon salt
- -1 teaspoon allspice
- -1 teaspoon nutmeg
- -2 teaspoons cinnamon
- -2 teaspoons baking soda
- -1 cup saffron oil
- -2 eggs

Directions

1. Preheat the oven to 350°F.
2. Peel and chop 3 ½ cups of apples.
3. In a bowl, mix apples and two cups of sugar, let sit for 10 minutes.
4. In a separate bowl sift together flour, salt, allspice, nutmeg, cinnamon, and baking soda.
5. Combine flour mixture with oil and two eggs.
6. Add apples and sugar to the flour mixture.
7. Pour into an oven-safe pan and bake for 50-60 minutes.

Jodi's Apple Cake

A collection of poems to describe my journey.

Content warning: Eating Disorders, Grief, Addiction

<u>I.</u>

<u>Just a poem</u>

As soon as he felt my pain
Is when he came.
I had pushed him aside
But now he is back along for the ride.
He lures me in
All you have to do is concentrate on being thin.
Starve yourself, no one will know
For you know all the secrets, so you can just go
And if by chance you have to eat
Then you know just where to go and who to meet
It only takes a moment, simply act on the urge
And purge.
50 pushups here 50 crunches there
Triceps biceps shoulder and back
Keep on going and you will continue to get near
Push your feelings away and numb yourself out
Put on a happy face and do not ever pout.
No need to thank me for I am just doing my job
And I have succeeded from making you sob.

<u>II.</u>

<u>How I felt as a kid</u>

Pick me up mama
Not now baby make me a picture
You are good at that
Pick me up mama
Not now I have to get ready
You pretend to get ready too
Pick me up mama

You are too big silly
Big girls don't need to be picked up

Hug me mama
Of course baby in a minute
Hug me mama
You don't want me to wrinkle
I'm going out
Hug me mama
Ok but I'm tired and sad could you hug me

Love me mama
You know I do and
You look so pretty today
Love me mama
I do love you but do you love me
Love me mama
I just bought you a pretty dress
Hear me mama
Don't ever lose your looks
Hear me mama
You have beautiful eyes
Hear me mama
I do hear you but I'm scared can't you hear me.

Hold me mama
Of course mama
Don't let go
I won't mommy
I can't do this without you
I'm right here you don't have to
Make it better
Of course I will mom

III.

After coming off pain pills
I was lost
I spent so many years in pain, I thought I was being strong but I was so very wrong.

I tried to put on a happy face and get through the day but it seemed someone had to pay.
I was no longer me and that I could not see
I wanted the pain to go away and so I let my soul stray.
I felt I could not catch a break and that was not fake
I couldn't function, I was coming to an impassable junction
Physically I was meek and weak, nauseous all the time but no one could see the sign
Emotionally it tore at my heart, not being able to be the me everyone used to see
My spirits were low even though I tried to stay on the go
Then my mother got sick and I felt this was a cruel trick
Once she was gone from this earth I was left with my grief, and I was not at peace
I was lost and in pain and felt I had nothing to gain
I was going through the daily motions trying not to make a commotion
I simply wanted the pain to end and I was not willing to bend
I began to withdraw from who I was, lost and alone was what gave me a buzz
I had a pill that took away my physical pain but left me with nothing to gain, I was so lost and at a great cost
I wanted to feel like and be the old me
When I tried and couldn't, I cried
So on my own and all alone I made my pain go away, but at what cost, again I was so very lost
This went on for a few years and looking back it puts me in tears and encompasses my fears
When I could hide everything was alright inside
I believe I hurt those around by being so curt,
I lost precious time at such a great cost, I was so lost.
I am happy to say that I have found my way
I pray that the people I love endured the wait and that I am not too late
I am no longer lost and hope that everyone can see I can now cope
There are days I am still in pain, but I realized my old ways of dealing left me nothing to gain
I still grieve the loss of my mother and a part of me that will never be
I am no longer lost, my eyes are wide open and my mind is clear I want to be everywhere
It's been a long drive but I am finally beginning to thrive
I know I have a ways to go but I am no longer so low
I am now embracing each day with clarity and hope and nope I will not look back
I will go forward with an appetite to live and to my loved ones continue to give

BIO

Jodi Capobianco is a stay-at-home mom who resides in Raynham, MA. In her spare time, Jodi volunteers with hospice patients, walks her dog, and enjoys going to the beach and using her peloton bike. She is a mom of five and an eating disorder survivor; she struggled specifically with restrictive anorexia and compulsive exercising.

Ingredients

-½ cup salted butter, melted
-1 cup graham cracker crumbs
-2 cups confectioners' sugar
-1 cup plus 2 tablespoons of peanut butter
-1 cup semi-sweet chocolate chips

Directions

1. Line an 8x8-inch square baking pan with foil or parchment paper.
2. Mix the melted butter, graham cracker crumbs, and confectioners' sugar together in a medium bowl.
3. Stir in one cup of peanut butter and press evenly in the baking pan.
4. Melt remaining two tablespoons of peanut butter with the chocolate chips in the microwave or on the stove. Stir until smooth.
5. Spread peanut butter and chocolate mixture over peanut butter layer.
6. Chill in the fridge until firm (at least 2 hours).
7. Allow to sit at room temperature for 10 minutes before cutting. Serve chilled. Setting them out for a few hours at room temperature is okay. Refrigerate bars when not eating, they will last for up to one week.

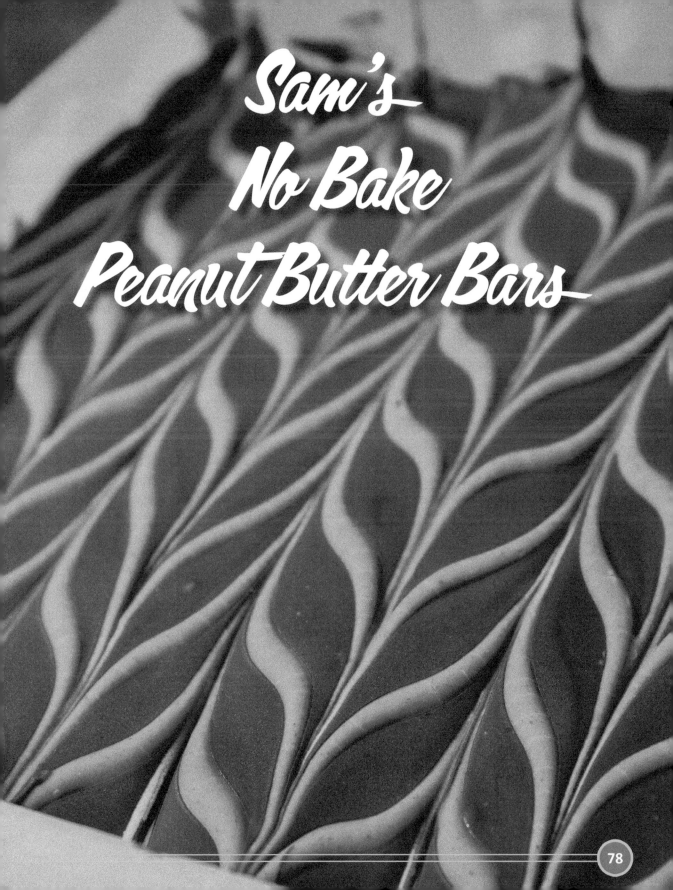

Sam's
No Bake
Peanut Butter Bars

Story

Having a sibling with diagnosed mental health challenges always made my own mental health feel less important or invisible. I always thought I was a people-pleaser and perfectionist by nature, but now I realize a lot of that had to do with this aspect of my story and my own mental health.

For a long time, I thought stress was equivalent to mental health. Mental health was never talked about as anything other than something negative in my community. I always viewed mental health as a form of failure. How could I have "mental health" if I didn't have a mental illness? Therefore, I managed things on my own.

This changed for me when I went to college. My parents divorced, a good friend of mine passed away unexpectedly, and my sibling who struggled with their mental health was at their most vulnerable. My only concept of therapy at the time was what I saw on TV and what I experienced through members of my family, which was always negative. I wasn't sure what to do. I knew something was wrong, I just didn't know what.

Also, being a man, I always associated therapy with weakness. I was told, "life's tough, wear a helmet," or, "toughen up," but what if what needs to be fixed isn't visible?

My perspective on therapy really shifted when I needed it the most. My anxiety manifests in physical symptoms, such as panic attacks, and I was having a hard time functioning without having someone help me manage these symptoms. After this, I saw a therapist for a while, and even though I knew I wasn't experiencing this alone, I still felt lonely. It wasn't until later that I realized that particular therapist may not have been the best fit. During a six-month hiatus from therapy, the panic attacks only became more frequent, so I looked for someone who could help me build skills to manage my anxiety rather than just talk therapy.

There is absolutely still a stigma attached to therapy, especially as a man. I am still working on detaching my own judgments about it, but I hope other men who read this know, it is okay to get help and it is okay to feel emotions, emotions don't make us weak; it just means we are human.

BIO

Sam Rogers is a software developer at meQuilibrium, an organization based in resilience and helping people find wellness in the workplace. Outside of work, he loves all things music, from playing the guitar to recording; he is even working on his own EP and produces the Beyond Measure Podcast. He also enjoys spending time with his girlfriend (the author of this book), chosen family, and biological family.

A World Without Suicide: Suicide Prevention

Suicide is the tenth-leading cause of death in the US and the second-leading cause of death for those ages ten to thirty-four. As hard as suicide can be to talk about, the more we discuss it, the less alone people who may be experiencing suicidal thoughts will feel and the more likely they may be to get help.

Although it may feel counterintuitive, asking someone directly if they are thinking about suicide can be life-saving. It is a common myth that asking someone directly will put the idea in their head, and while this is totally an understandable fear, this is statistically not true.

Additionally, those who die by suicide often exhibit warning signs, so it is important we all become educated on what these can look like. The following are some examples:

Talking about wanting to die (even in jest)
Exhibiting unbearable emotional or physical pain
Making a plan or researching ways to die
Withdrawing from loved ones and giving things away
Eating or sleeping more or less

It is incredibly hard to see a loved one struggling with suicidal thoughts and ideations. And it can be easy to feel responsible for helping the person struggling. While you can support the person in finding help and validating their feelings, it is important to remember that your role in their life is as a friend or family member, not a professional, and having you in their life, just as you are, is incredibly important and that is enough.

Lastly, the language we use when we talk about mental health and suicide is extremely important in destigmatizing mental illness. For this reason, it is important to replace "they committed suicide" with "they died by suicide." Committed infers this as a crime or choice, when really, when someone dies by suicide, it is at the hands of mental illness. This subtle change can make a big impact.

If you or someone you know is dealing with suicidal thoughts or actions, there is help available. Call the National Suicide Prevention Lifeline at 1-800-273-8255 or text "HOME" to 741-741 for the Crisis Textline.

For many people, death by suicide is not a will to die but rather an inability to see a way to live or to keep going. Suicide is preventable with the right actions, the work toward decreasing stigma, and the more we understand the warning signs. Do your part; let's create a world without suicide.

Overcoming Obstacles and Becoming Triumphant on the Other Side

Author's Voice: As people on planet earth, each one of us has experienced some type of obstacle and/or pain. And while I wish I could take the suffering away from each of us, I know these feelings are not only unifying, but also necessary. Obstacles and challenges are undeniable parts of life, regardless of your disposition, life circumstances, or mental health... We all experience pain at some point. The good news is that we are capable of feeling just the opposite, too! Experiencing joy, gratitude, and peace are only amplified when it comes after a difficult experience.

The other piece of this is that the resilience of the human spirit is just so cool! To know we are all faced with challenges that we feel will only break us... We work to heal and move forward each time, and that is inspiring!

Although we all feel these feelings and experience pain to some degree, I want to point out that "there is no comparison of misery." In my own journey managing my depression, and also in healing from a sexual assault, I have often felt "things could have been worse, so I don't 'deserve' to feel this way..." Well, I have learned you feel what you feel and you have every right to those feelings, regardless of the person next to you. Sure, we may all imagine someone else could have it "worse," but that does not change or negate our suffering or feelings.

I applaud and appreciate those who shared their struggles here and hope that as you read them, you feel inspired rather than defeated. You are just as deserving of help and happiness, as well as pride, for moving forward despite what you have faced; let these stories lead the way.

Ingredients

-2 cups all-purpose flour
-2 tablespoons loose Earl Grey tea leaves
-½ teaspoon salt
-¾ cup confectioners' sugar
-1 teaspoon pure vanilla extract
-1 cup (2 sticks) butter, room temperature

Directions

1. In a food processor, pulse together the flour, tea, and salt, until the tea is just spotted throughout the flour.
2. Add the confectioners' sugar, vanilla, and butter. Pulse together just until a dough is formed.
3. Place dough on a sheet of plastic wrap and chill in the refrigerator for 30 minutes.
4. Preheat the oven to 375°F.
5. Slice the log into 1/3 inch-thick discs.
6. Place on parchment-lined baking sheets, 2 inches apart.
7. Bake until the edges are just brown, about 12 minutes.
8. Let cool on sheet for 5 minutes, then transfer to wire racks and cool to room temperature.

Hannah L.'s Earl Grey Shortbread Cookies

Recipe pulled from the Food Network

Story

Do you constantly seek approval and affirmation?
Do you fail to recognize your accomplishments?
Do you fear criticism?
Do you overextend yourself?
Have you had problems with your own compulsive behavior?
Do you have a need for perfection?
Are you uneasy when your life is going smoothly, continually anticipating problems?
Do you feel more alive in the midst of a crisis?
Do you feel responsible for others?
Do you care for others easily, yet find it difficult to care for yourself?
Do you isolate yourself from other people?
Do you respond with fear to authority figures and angry people?
Do you feel that individuals and society in general are taking advantage of you?
Do you have trouble with intimate relationships?
Do you confuse pity with love?
Do you attract and/or seek people who tend to be compulsive and/or abusive?
Do you cling to relationships because you are afraid of being alone?
Do you often mistrust your own feelings and the feelings expressed by others?
Do you find it difficult to identify and express your emotions?
Do you think someone else's addiction may have affected you?
If you answered "yes" to most or all of the questions above, you may benefit from an Anon recovery program.

These are the questions that convinced me to start my journey to recovery from the effects of addiction on my life. I read them after being strongly encouraged by my therapist to check out this program for the family and friends of addicted people, sort of like a support group. My father is an alcoholic and has been active in his addiction from the time I was seven years old. He started attending AA meetings when I was twenty-one, which is only about a year ago as of the writing of this essay. He still struggles with sobriety.

Despite having been raised in the dysfunction of addiction, I was also knowingly in a relationship with another addict—though I thought he was sober at the time. And this therapist was not the first person to recommend an Anon program to me after learning of my father's and partner's afflictions. Apparently, I had a "high-threshold" for addiction-tolerance.

I had shrugged off these suggestions before, but this time was different. I was working remotely through the Covid-19 pandemic, living in a basement with no windows, in a city where I only knew my roommates and had very little socialization outside of my romantic partnership. It was January—cold, dark, and gray—and I felt isolated and depressed. I was considering applying for a promotion, but a voice inside told me I wasn't likable enough for a leadership position. This thought struck me so powerfully, and I believed it so thoroughly, that I had a tiny breakdown as a result. And then I was upset with myself. Hadn't I been in therapy for two years, working on loving myself? Why was I still stuck here?

Vulnerable and desperate for anything to help me climb out of the hole I'd spiraled into, I told my therapist I would look into the recovery program. I did a quick Google search and found the quiz above. I was shocked to find most of the traits I believed were "just me" on the list. I had never considered they may have been coping strategies developed in response to my dad's addiction. I had never considered there may be others like me

It was around this time I also started attending a free mindfulness meditation group called Still Together, which met at a local library in the pre-pandemic past and was currently meeting weekly on Zoom. The first session ended with a "loving kindness" meditation, in which we were guided to picture ourselves as small children, hold our younger selves, and say our names. "Hannah," I whispered, my hand on my heart. "May you be happy and feel loved, healthy and feel strong, safe and feel protected, and at peace, and feel satisfied and content." The meditation had me shaking with quiet sobs. I didn't know how starved I had been for my own affection. Instead of loving and nurturing the sweet little girl I saw in my mind, I was telling her she was unattractive, unlikable, unlovable, unworthy. I needed to do something different.

That was the beginning of this current phase of my healing, and I started working an Anon recovery program. Just in time, too, because about a month later, my partner revealed to me that he was not as sober as he had led me to believe. His disclosure brought me to my knees. My trust was shattered, insecurities amplified, fear and catastrophizing gripping me moment after moment. I had arrived at that infamous rock bottom.

My partner entered his own recovery program, and I doubled down in mine. I attended as many meetings as I could, got a sponsor, and started working the steps. Anon programs are modeled after AA and other 12 Step programs, on the principle that addiction is a "family disease." I did my best to be honest, open-minded, and willing to trust the process. I told myself the devastation would pass. That I would grow from this experience. That time would mend. And, sure enough, I started to see changes after some time. I was learning and growing. I experienced peace of mind. I recovered the feeling of joy.

As I discovered these new ways of thinking and doing, I began to feel better and healthier. At the same time, I was asked by Paulette, the leader of Still Together, if I would be interested in reading some poetry at the next session, since I had been a regular attendee of the group for a few months at that point. Every third week of the month is a "mashup" session, in which members of the group contribute by leading various meditations or reading a poem they admire. Paulette added that if I wanted to write an original poem for the session, that would be most welcome.

I was excited at the opportunity to write again. I had lost my drive to create since finishing my Creative Writing undergraduate program, and poetry has always been a favorite form of catharsis for me. I'm no Dickinson, and that's fine by me. I don't need my poems to be great. I just need them to express my joy, my pain, my confliction, my serenity.
So, I wrote a poem. And the next month, I wrote another one. My poetry has since become part of the fabric of our mashup meditation sessions. I'm so grateful to have a reason to write again, and to have a place to share these pieces of my heart. It has revived my creative spirit. And now I am grateful for the chance to share some of these poems with you.

<u>the players</u>

am I the hero of my story?
if so, which version of me
gets the credit?

my mind is crowded
with leading ladies
elbowing for the spotlight.

there's mama hen,
who clucks and worries
and takes care of
everyone but herself.

the queen is hard to please
and longs to be revered by all.
no one lives up to her expectations,
least of all herself.

the ghost haunts the house of grief,
moving from room to room.
she cannot stay in acceptance long enough
to find the door to freedom.

the smallest is a five-year-old girl
with pigtails and a pale blue dress.
she only wants to be held and told
that she is loved right here, right now.

these are the players
who tell my story,
whether I asked them to or not.

there are no villains,
only armored hearts
forged in fear and difficult to remove—
but not impossible.

maybe I am not the hero of my story.
maybe I'm the playwright;
I decide who gets the lines
and who waits quietly off stage.

I decide when to take the armor off
and thank the players
for getting me through the first act.

it's time to introduce
some new characters.
watch this space for act ii.

Real, But Not True

I am a powerful storyteller
I have loved to tell stories
from a young age

I used to write about
monsters and dragons
and utopian societies

But none of my creations
were ever as captivating

as the stories I told myself

It's scary, sometimes,
how convincing I can be,
labeling fantasy as nonfiction

No wonder I have lived
from fear instead of love
No wonder I stopped
listening to my soul

I am such a powerful storyteller
that my stories
have become my reality

and the part of me that knows
the truth in all things
is drowned by the voice
telling me to abandon my truth

Whenever I think I'm done
believing these stories,
I fall for it again
and am left angry and afraid,
the wind knocked out of me

What keeps hope alive
in my heart is picking myself up
and filling my lungs again

I pay attention to my stories
and the kooky narrator
who makes them up

I thank her for her input and
put a new label on the cover:
real, but not true

Future Self

I sit with her in the garden.

She did it.
She made my dream her reality:
flowers and vegetables
of all colors and shapes,
blooming in vibrant
reds and yellows and pinks.

We sit on a bench
surrounded by lilac bushes.
They smell like childhood.
Her cats, in their orange
and white and grey coats,
rub themselves on my legs,
their purrs audible
even in the breeze.

She has long brown hair
streaked with gray:
silver foxy.
Her arms and waist
are thicker than mine,
her skin is not as taut.
Age has rounded and stretched her,
and she has never been more beautiful.

I lay my head in her lap
as she strokes my hair
and listens to my heart
as it pours out:
all the fears and anxieties,
the resentments,
the pain and grief
of this moment in my life.

"Do you remember?" I ask her,
"How did you get through it?"
She looks at me with my kind brown eyes.
They are radiant in the sunlight.
She strokes my hair some more.
Her lap is thick and soft.
I feel safe here.

"I remember some," she says.
"Most of it has disappeared behind me,
And I don't look too hard for it."
I tell her that the storm
seems to be here permanently.
But even as I speak,
I notice how this moment here,
in the garden with the cats,
is also stretching forever.

"This too shall bless," she tells me.
"You will survive and grow stronger,
and you won't wish
for anything to be different.
Oh, my darling," she smiles,
her cheeks creasing with the
familiar expression of joy,
"you have no idea what's coming."

BIO

Hannah Little was born and raised in Vermont. She has always loved storytelling in all its forms. She earned a BFA in Creative Writing from Roger Williams University in 2020, where she also studied theater and arts management. She now lives in Providence, RI, where she serves her community and works to keep creativity and the arts alive.

Ingredients

- 1 package baker's semisweet chocolate
- 1 ½ cups shredded coconut

Directions

1. Line a cookie sheet with wax paper.
2. Melt the chocolate in a saucepan over very low heat, stirring constantly.
3. Add the coconut and mix until completely covered.
4. Drop by teaspoons onto wax paper.
5. Chill and enjoy.

Eve's Haystacks

Story

At eighty-one years old, I feel grateful that I have led a fairly stable life. My husband and I were married when I was eighteen and he was twenty,—babies by today's standards, and yet we raised three children and they went on to have eight amazing children of their own. Life is certainly a rollercoaster, and it took me a while to realize that eventually all will work out the way it should. It is hard to believe that, though, when you are in the midst of difficult circumstances, and I noticed this especially when I watched two people very close to me deal with depression. In both situations, it was frustrating for me to try and understand. It was also hard for me not to feel as though it was my fault. One person had attempted to end her life, but she was able to get help. After the suicide attempt, she was taken to the emergency room, where a doctor said, "Slap a ticket on her and ship her to (the psychiatric hospital I have since forgotten the name of)." She lived there for a while and was told to write her life story. When I went to see her on visiting day, I remember she was placed in a circle with other residents and told to bang on a tambourine. She got up and walked out. The nurses panicked, wondering if they should put her on "suicide watch," but knowing she was a classically trained musician, I could understand why she got upset. In fact, I was happy to see it; she was becoming herself again!

In the other case, the person was dealing with terminal illness and in my eyes, he had every reason to be depressed. He was told to fill out "state-of-mind questionnaires," as he experienced both depression and paralyzing fear. When he passed away, I was left with an immense amount of grief and sadness myself. I often heard well-meaning people in my life say, "He is in a better place" (really, have you been there?), "You will feel better in a year," (wrong!), "Soon the good memories will replace the memories of the final illness," (wrong again!), and so it goes. I finally realized that this is *me* facing an unbelievable loss and everything I felt and continue to feel is okay. I had to learn how to handle finances, how to cook for one, and how to face the fears at night when I heard a strange noise in my house. And I had to learn how to live with a part of my heart missing.

Do I still experience my own depression? Of course! There still is at times, but I accept it as a part of an ongoing process. I look at the good things in my life and know that he is watching over me. Do I still cry when I hear Joe Cocker sing "You are So Beautiful"? Yes! Fifteen years later, I still do, because he sang that to me all the time.

Am I over it? No, I will never be; I have just learned how to live with grief. It would be impossible to keep up with the intensity of grief that I experienced in the first weeks and months, so it has been a quiet part of me that will always be there, and I am learning that is okay.

BIO

Eve Altman is eighty-one years old. A widow, a mother of three, and a grandmother of eight, one of whom is the awesome author of this book. Eve loves to read, color (on the happy color app), crochet, watch TV, and learn new technology. She tries to enjoy every minute of this life that is whizzing by at a very fast pace.

Ingredients

-1 box cake mix and ingredients listed on the box
-2 cans frosting
-1 bag candy melts
-1 container sprinkles
-Optional: nuts, other small candies for outside of cake pops

Directions

1. Using a cake mix, create cake and bake.
2. Once baked and cooled, break up the cake into fine crumbs. You can do this by putting the cake in a stand mixer with a paddle attachment, a food processor, or by using your hands.
3. Take your cans of favorite frosting and add it to the cake mixture. Dive into the cake crumbs with your clean hands and mix the frosting with the cake crumbs (you can also use gloves if you want or go back to the mixer).
4. Measure out cake balls (about 1 tablespoon-worth of cake) and knead with your hands to make it round. Put the cake ball on parchment paper, tray, or plate.
5. Using the microwave, melt candy melts for one minute and stir until chocolate is completely melted.
6. Dip the cake pop stick into the chocolate and then your cake ball, put in the fridge for ten minutes to set.
7. Once set, dip the entire cake ball in more melted chocolate.
8. Dip cake balls completely in chocolate and decorate with sprinkles, candies, or nuts. The chocolate dries quickly so be quick if adding decorations.

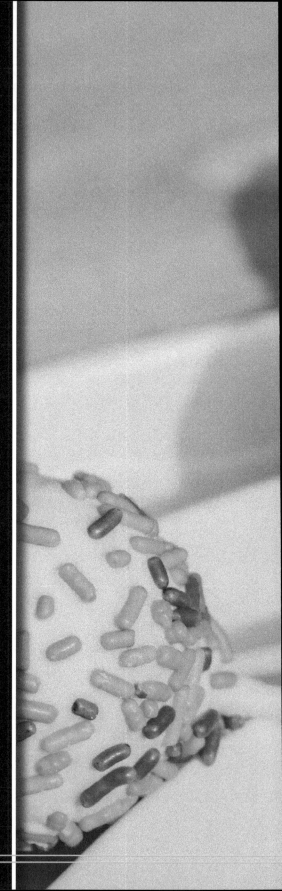

Clarisse's Cake Pops

Story

   I always hear people tell beautiful stories about how nice it is to sleep when it is raining outside. This, however, was never something I could relate to, especially for the first nine years of my life. Until I moved to the United States, it was impossible for me to sleep through the rain. I lived in the capital city of Cameroon (Central Africa) with my family until I was nine years old. We lived in an impoverished neighborhood plagued with constant floods every time it rained, especially during the rainy season, which lasted for four months during a good year and six or more months during a bad year. The water tables were very high where we lived, and as a result, we experienced frequent flooding. Almost every time it rained, we would attempt to gather as many items off the ground as physically possible. Still, there was never enough time, so as a result, we would lose a significant amount of our property because the water destroyed almost everything it touched.

Initially, I relied on my parents and elder siblings to secure our property and carry me to safety. I didn't become directly involved in the process of protecting our house, property, and my siblings from the wrath of the floods until my father immigrated to the United States, my elder siblings went to boarding school, and my mom got a job out of state. One day I was a nine-year-old, and the next day I was a nine-year-old who was responsible for her two younger siblings and literally keeping the house afloat. This experience changed my life significantly and shaped me into who I am today.

Carrying our belongings to safety, I found strength that I did not know was there. At that moment, I was only thinking of my family and my property, not the fact that I was just a kid. I had to put my fears away and put on a brave face for my younger siblings. When I walked into the water, I told myself that everything was going to be alright, and everything was or became alright because failure wasn't an option. My family's safety was on the line, and I was responsible for them. To date, I have the same conviction when I face difficulties, either in school or in my personal life. As a result, I never back down from a challenge.

 In addition to learning how to be strong, I learned how to be a leader. Every time it flooded, I moved my younger siblings and made sure that everybody was secure. This taught me how to take charge of situations, and ever since then, leadership has come naturally to me. Once moving to the United States, I sought leadership positions in classes and programs that I was a part of, like at Girls Incorporated of Lynn. At Girls Inc., I was an ambassador who gave tours and spoke at events for donors. Every time I got up in front of an audience, I did so confidently. I talked about the importance of leading by action in my speeches and how Girls Inc. helped improve my leadership skills and mold me into the independent woman I am today. Now I attend Boston College as a freshman and seek out similar opportunities.

Frequently seeing my family picture albums, clothes, and books get washed away by the floods frightened me even more than the water. It was as though if we all died, no one would ever know we existed. As traumatic as this experience might have been, it has helped transform and shape me into the intelligent, strong, resilient, confident, and independent woman I am today.

BIO

Clarisse Ebeh is a freshman at Boston College. She moved to the US from Cameroon, Africa, in the fall of 2015. Her adventurous and curious personality drove her to participate in all kinds of programs when she arrived in the US, such as Girls Inc. of Lynn, The Food Project, Upward Bound (college readiness program), and LaVida Scholars. An aspiring pediatric oncologist, Clarisse is passionate about health and building community and is excited about what the future holds for her.

Ingredients

-6 tablespoons butter, divided
-1 package (11 ½ ounces) milk chocolate chips
-2 ounces unsweetened chocolate (if this is not available, you can simply use 2 ounces more of the chocolate chips)
-1 can (14 ounces) sweetened condensed milk
-¼ cup crushed candy canes (about 3), or more if you'd like
-1 teaspoon mint extract
-16 Oreo cookies
-1 ½ cups miniature marshmallows

Directions

1. Line an 8-inch square baking pan with foil or parchment paper, letting ends extend up sides; grease foil with 2 tablespoons of butter (or until it is covered).
2. In a microwave-safe bowl, melt the chocolate and remaining 4 tablespoons of butter; stir until smooth. Add condensed milk, crushed candy canes, and mint extract. Stir until blended.
3. Pour half the mixture into the prepared pan.
4. Arrange Oreo cookies over chocolate, cutting to fit as needed.
5. Stir marshmallows into remaining chocolate mixture and spread over cookies. Refrigerate until firm, about 1 hour.
5. Using the foil or parchment, lift the fudge out of the pan. Remove the foil and cut fudge into roughly 1-inch squares.
6. Store between layers of waxed paper in a container.

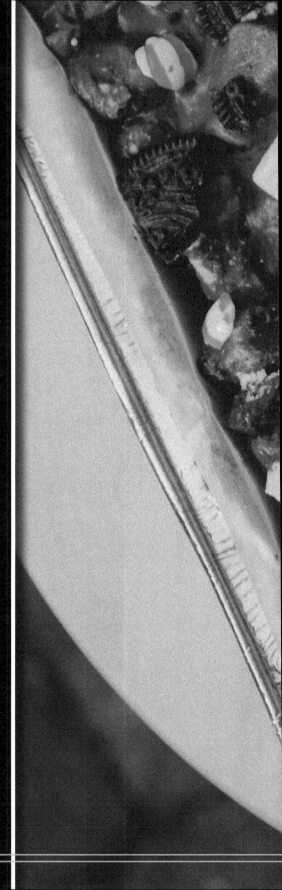

Shannon's Minty Cookies & Cream Chocolate Fudge

Story

Family does not mean those who are related to you by DNA, but those who are there for you when times get hard. My parents got divorced when I was six months old, and at nine months old, my mother met my step-father. They got married when I was four, and my step-brother split his time with them and his mother. My sister and I were allowed to see our mother every other weekend, based on the order of the court. Money and manipulation can get you everywhere in this world, including time with your children. My father raised my sister and I, denying us any opportunity to see our mother. She would drive to his house each day to get us ready in the morning while he slept in with his new girlfriend. Life was a mess to begin with. As I grew older, the expectations of being a genius daughter became overwhelming. If I came home with any grade less than a 100%, I was asked, "What happened?" and told, "Next time, try harder." I dedicated my life to schoolwork in hopes that I wouldn't become a failure. Come fifth grade, the depression and anxiety hit hard, with no way to stop it. I was still infrequently allowed to visit my mother and days with my father became more stressful and tense. My step-brother was in and out of jail, battling with drugs and dropping out of school. My sixth-grade teacher recognized my pain and became my only friend. Seventh grade came and the hatred I had for myself grew. I stopped eating, worked out excessively, and cried myself to sleep each night. I couldn't take the pressure, the high expectations, the awful school I was in. I wanted to end it all and I almost did.

My parents went back to court so my sister and I could change our address and live with our mom, but the court process takes a couple of years. It was in eighth grade I found out my sister had been cutting herself for three years, and my mom became obsessed with her health and wellbeing. Meanwhile, I was still struggling to get up in the morning and find the will to breathe, but I kept a smile on my face.

It came to the point that I never wanted to be at my father's house. The yelling, swearing, high expectations, putting me down, it was too much. He told me I would never succeed, my dream of being a teacher was pointless, and I would never do anything meaningful with my life.

One night, I called my sister, asking her to pick me up because I wanted to go home to my mom's house. As I walked past my father without saying a word, he ran to the door and blocked me from leaving. My sister was outside waiting in the car, but I was physically unable to move my father away from the door. I reached for the door handle and he grabbed my wrist, not letting go. I screamed at the top of my lungs for him to stop touching me and to let me go. My sister heard my screams and opened the door from the outside, grabbed my hand, and I ran out. My father shouted at us saying he was going to call the police, put an Amber Alert out for me, and have my sister arrested for kidnapping. On the car ride home, we called our mother and told her what happened. I spoke to the police that night for the first time. Of course, that report went nowhere, and after talking with DCYF (Division for Children, Youth, and Families), they decided it was not a significant enough event to mention in the court battle.

My sister was graduating high school that year, so the court case was really for me to move schools and live with my mother. Eventually, my mother was able to gain custody, and the incident that occurred was never spoken of again. I refused to follow the court schedule of when I should see my father, which caused serious issues in my family. My aunts, uncles, cousins, and grandparents stopped talking to me, and they still don't. I was blocked on Facebook from my grandmother, simply for wanting to live with my mother. My sister and I went back to my father's house one day, grabbed everything we could, and left. I've only ever been back once. During this time, I began dating the most incredible person, who helped me each day with my internal struggles, even though he lived two states away. I began to self-harm and the depression and anxiety continued to worsen. As high school continued, my boyfriend stayed by my side and never let me struggle alone. He was the one who helped me stop cutting and has continued to be my biggest support. School was still incredibly stressful, and I have never been able to think anything less than a 100% is okay. When it came time to find a college, I was told by family members that I needed to go to Harvard. Anything less, and it wouldn't be worth it. I was smart and I should go to a school that shows that. As someone who wanted to be a teacher, I decided Harvard was not the college for me, and I found my place at Southern New Hampshire University (SNHU). My father and grandparents were extremely disappointed in my decision, and I was told that since I did not choose Harvard, my life was not worth living. I am reminded of this every day I do my schoolwork, and I continue to struggle with my image, confidence, internal thoughts, stress, and wanting to continue life.

I am forever grateful for my boyfriend who is still with me, and my best friend, as they are the only ones I trust. They are the only people who know about my struggles. My sister was recently diagnosed with borderline personality disorder, and my mother continues to spend all of her energy making sure she is okay.

My family has no idea about anything I have ever struggled with. I have never been diagnosed with anything or even told my doctor about how I've felt. I cannot say for certain that I have depression, anxiety, or struggled with an eating disorder because I don't know if it would be true. I have suffered in silence for eight years, with only two people knowing the true me. Baking is actually one of the places where I feel true joy and know it is okay to make mistakes and mess up. Although life can be challenging and it brings you to your weakest point, just know that you are strong, you are beautiful inside and out, you are brave, and you can do this. I believe in you.

Bio

Shannon is a current sophomore at Southern New Hampshire University, majoring in elementary education and general special education, and minoring in mathematics. She hopes to become an educator that promotes and celebrates students' differences in her classroom. She is currently starting to create a mental health curriculum to be used in elementary schools for her Honors Thesis. Originally from New Hampshire, she hopes to earn her Master's Degree in education after graduating with her Bachelor's Degree from SNHU. Outside of school, she loves to bake, sing, paint, and spend time with those closest to her.

Ingredients

-8 tablespoons whole-milk plain Greek yogurt
-1 cup brown sugar
-1 teaspoon vanilla extract
-2 beaten eggs
-3 very ripe mashed bananas
-½ teaspoon salt
-1 teaspoon baking soda
-1 teaspoon cinnamon
-¼ teaspoon allspice
-1 ¼ cups unbleached all-purpose flour
-½ cup dark chocolate chunks/chips

Directions

1. Preheat the oven to 350°F.
2. Cream yogurt and brown sugar together in a large bowl.
3. Stir in vanilla, eggs, and banana.
4. Slowly sift in salt, baking soda, cinnamon, all spice, and flour.
5. Mix gently until combined.
6. Fold in dark chocolate chunks/chips.
7. Pour into a muffin tin.
8. Bake in the oven for 20-25 minutes, checking every 5-10 minutes until they are done.
9. Muffins are done when a toothpick inserted at the center comes out mostly clean.
10. Carefully pop out of the pan and place on a wire rack to cool.

Beth's Chocolate Chip Banana Muffins

Get Back Up Again

Get Back Up Again

Five years is an incredibly long time when you really think about it. If you'd asked me five years ago where I would be today, I can honestly say that I would not have guessed anywhere close to my current reality. At the end of 2016, I was still living at home with my mom and my senior dog, Rusty, dating a completely different person, and was only a few months into my first "big kid" job out of college, all without the slightest idea of how drastically 2017 was about to turn my entire life upside down.

The beginning of 2017 began pretty normally, to be fair; I was working and spending most of my free time with my boyfriend of almost two years, and we had even talked about finding an apartment that would allow my dog. Everything seemed to be heading in a good direction. A few months into the year, however, Rusty's health took a turn to the point where he was struggling to walk, and after several vet visits, it was determined that the best thing we could do for him was to keep him comfortable and that it was only a matter of time before we would have to say goodbye. Sadly, that time came sooner than later and we had to help Rusty cross the rainbow bridge in mid-June, just a few weeks before my boyfriend and I were scheduled to go on a trip out of state for his cousin's wedding.

We had to pick up Rusty's ashes the day we left for the four-day wedding trip, then began what turned out to be a hellish twenty-four-hour drive south. Exhausted, we arrived at our Airbnb in the wee hours of the morning and immediately crashed. The next day, we discovered that his car had blown a transmission line during the long drive and what little fluid was left had leaked onto the driveway while we slept. The trip only got worse from there... It was the kind of vacation from hell where everything that could go wrong did go wrong, from bad communication and cramped quarters down to really small details, like my flip flop breaking while walking to our seats at the wedding. We were ultimately forced to extend our trip so the car could be repaired, thus missing an extra two days of work. When we finally got home, my boyfriend and I had to immediately go to my coworker's house to house-sit while she was on vacation for the Fourth of July, as we had promised several weeks prior to do so.

With tensions from the bad vacation still somewhat lingering between us, we went back to our respective jobs and stayed at the house caring for my coworker's cats, but at the time, I had no reason to believe that the tension wouldn't blow over. At the end of the week, we both went back to our own homes, and while things still felt a bit strained, after nearly two and a half years together, I felt confident things would go back to normal in a week or so. Boy, was I wrong.

By the next afternoon, I was reeling, rug ripped out from under me, as my boyfriend of two and a half years, who I had expected to be building a life with, suddenly broke up with me via text message. I was furious and hurt and confused and about ten other emotions I couldn't identify as I tried desperately to understand how my life had gone from awesome to awful in just a few short months. How did the one person I believed I could count on outside of my biological relatives become a stranger and someone who only resembled the guy I had thought I would marry someday just a few days prior? After a lot of confusing back and forth with him waffling over his words, ultimately not making much sense, and me grappling to understand where this was all coming from, he agreed to meet with me at a restaurant that weekend. I barely ate or slept that week as I performed my job like a zombie and wracked my brain for clues as to where I had gone wrong in this relationship.

The meet-up was fifty shades of horrifying, to say the least. I sat across the table from this stranger, wanting to simultaneously hit him and hug him as he babbled on about how he suddenly didn't love me anymore. Although, it was actually only sudden for me, because he had apparently known for six-plus months before that point that he didn't love me, and he just didn't know how to say it. I kept my face as blank as possible as I alternated between staring at the center of his forehead and at the wall behind his head, because I couldn't bear to look into the eyes of the person who had lied to my face for *months,* just because he was too much of a coward to be honest with a girl who had only ever loved him with her whole heart. I could only hear about half the words that were falling out of his mouth onto the table between us, like pellets of hail on pavement, over the thudding in my ears as my heart pounded with anxiety and exhaustion. After what felt like hours of him going back and forth about how he felt and what he wanted, which only further confused the matter as far as I was concerned, our strange and uncomfortable meeting came to a close with a promise to meet up again for coffee in September to "reassess."

I spent the majority of the summer of 2017 as a depressed husk of a person who barely slept or ate and robotically went about life on autopilot as my brain relentlessly combed over every moment of my now-deceased relationship. Analyzing how it all went so wrong, as if finding the answers in the past could somehow relieve my present pain, but it didn't. The only thing that made a difference was one day, when I went to visit my aunt, and we embarked on a creative journey to discover acrylic pouring. I began making the hour-long drive to her house almost every weekend so we could play with new methods of applying the paint on different substrates to our hearts' content during the day, then snuggle up on the couch with her little dog Bella in the evening to watch Haven on Netflix until we couldn't keep our eyes open. The long drives to my aunt's became cathartic as I would roll down the windows and blast my carefully crafted breakup playlist in my '96 Volkswagen Jetta named Rosaline. I belted out the lyrics in my concert for one, as if those songs of heartache were written just for me, and by the time I reached my aunt's front door I felt ready to let it all go and play with some paint. This went on for several months; over that time, I started eating and sleeping like a normal human again, for the most part, and although I was still hurting, I had finally started to feel like me again. By this time, September rolled around, and then it was time for the "reassessment" coffee meeting.

He had texted a few days prior to agree on a location, and after months of silence, it was jarring to hear that text message tone chime on my phone once again. He let me choose the coffee shop and I decided on one that I wouldn't care about ever going to again because I didn't really think constant reminders would be good for my mental health at that point. On the way there, I blasted my new female empowerment playlist and tried to consider what I was walking into. I wasn't really sure what would happen at this bizarre meeting and I wasn't even sure I knew what I wanted to happen, but I did know that one way or another I needed something conclusive.

I arrived fifteen minutes early, hoping to be able to get a seat and settle in before he showed up, but he apparently had the same idea and was already there waiting for me. I took a few deep breaths, smoothed my hair, and then walked as confidently as I could into the coffee shop and sat down across from him. We exchanged awkward pleasantries and small talk before he seemed to pick right back up where he left off several months prior, contradicting himself with every other sentence. I sat there staring at this stranger as he babbled on about how he was still glad we broke up but that he wanted to stay friends because I was a nice person and he has always stayed friends with his exes. So I asked him three separate times to give me an actually good reason for why he wanted to be my friend, but he just kept repeating the same two bogus reasons with different words in slightly varied order, until I finally realized I didn't care.

With refreshed determination, I stood up from the table and turned to tell him that I was leaving because I didn't belong there anymore and neither did he. Confidently, I walked out of the shop as he stared after me, dumbfounded. A few feet from my car, I remembered that I had some things he left at my house in the trunk, so I was starting to pull them out as he came out of the coffee shop. I handed him a bag of clothes but hesitated on the last item, which was a nearly full bottle of expensive rum we had purchased on that terrible vacation. I looked at him and explained that I didn't want to keep it but I really didn't want him to have it either. To me it wasn't about the rum as much as it was how the rum had become a representation for the last huge spoonful of lies he fed me before dumping me. We stood there awkwardly for a moment as I considered what to do, since you can't just randomly hand a stranger an open bottle of rum... then it came to me.

He followed me curiously as I walked over to the edge of the parking lot, bottle in hand, then I watched as the confusion on his face melted into shocked disappointment when I unscrewed the cap and poured the entire bottle of alcohol out onto the grass beside us. He followed the last drop to the ground with his bewildered eyes while I screwed the cap back on, then I pushed the empty bottle into his chest and told him to have a nice life. In an instant I was back in my car, windows down, music blasting a song that fit the moment perfectly, as I drove confidently out of the parking lot heading for the highway that would take me to my aunt's house for another therapeutic painting weekend.

I know, I know... That epic conclusion sounds like something you'd only see in the movies, but I swear it happened just like that, and from it came the exact closure I needed to move on with my life. And move on I certainly did, because by the end of that year, I became a homeowner at age twenty-four, and by January of 2018, I was living on my own in a new city, which was ironic considering that in the end, one of my ex's big complaints about our relationship was that "nothing would ever change." Joke's on you, bud. Fast forward to February of 2018, when I finally found the courage to stick my toe back into the dating pool and I briefly dated a sweet, slightly older guy, who reminded me that good ones are out there. It ultimately didn't work out with us, but that brief experience with someone who treated me really well was enough to give me the confidence to actually ask someone out for the first time ever that June.

Little did I know it would be the first and last time I would ask anyone out, since after two and a half years of dating, he proposed in October of 2019, and we have now been married since the end of December 2020. But I guess that leads us back to where we started, doesn't it? Five-years-ago me would never have guessed that I would be sitting here writing this story at my desk in the home office of the house I bought on my own at the end of the very same year my entire life seemed like it was ending... where I now live with my loving husband, Joe, our adorable cat, Izzy and our eight fascinating pet garden snails. (Yes, garden snails!)

The moral of the story here is to say... never count yourself out. I am living proof that just when you think you've hit the lowest point imaginable, you might just find a trampoline that rockets you back to a better, higher place than you've ever been or ever thought you could be. That's not to say that my life is perfect, of course; these last couple years of pandemic insanity and being unemployed have certainly been a struggle for me, one that I am still working to regain balance from. But honestly, writing this story has reminded me that if 2017 me could weather that whole shitstorm and come out stronger for it, 2021 me is gonna rock this shiz when she's good and ready, and when she does... It's going to be awesome!

BIO:
Beth Testa is a surface pattern designer and a badass twenty-eight-plus-year survivor of this crazy thing called life. A lover of all things retro, funky, and vintage, especially if it is classic-Volkswagen-related, she has a growing collection of eight-track tapes (that she actually listens to) and drives a standard car because it's way more fun. Beth is a wife to her amazing husband, Joe, and the proud mama of her feline fur daughter, Izzy, and eight pet garden snails that she affectionately calls her shell children. She loves to bake, listen to audiobooks, and is highly skilled at the art of crafting Spotify playlists for every mood and occasion.

Ingredients

-1 ⅓ cups flour
-½ teaspoon baking soda
-½ teaspoon salt
-6 tablespoons unsalted butter, room temperature
-½ cup granulated sugar
-1 large egg, room temperature
-2 tablespoons vanilla extract
-⅓ cup buttermilk
-2 cups confectioners' sugar
-2 teaspoons lemon juice
-2 tablespoons water (plus more as needed)
-1 tablespoon light corn syrup
-½ teaspoon vanilla extract
-3 tablespoons cocoa powder
-1 teaspoon corn starch

Directions

1. Preheat the oven to 350°F.
2. Combine flour, salt, and baking soda in a bowl and whisk together.
3. In a separate bowl or using a stand mixer, cream the butter and sugar until light and fluffy.
4. Mix in the egg and 2 tablespoons of vanilla until combined.
5. Add the flour mixture and buttermilk in alternating batches, starting and ending with flour; mix until combined.
6. Drop balls of batter onto a lined baking sheet 4 inches apart, as they spread in the oven.
7. Bake at 350°F for 13-14 minutes.
8. Let cookies cool upside down so the bottom becomes the flat top to ice.
9. In a bowl, combine confectioners' sugar, ½ teaspoon of vanilla, lemon juice, corn syrup, and water, mixing until smooth.
10. Transfer half the icing to a separate bowl and add 3 tablespoons of cocoa powder, a teaspoon of corn starch, and a few teaspoons of water.
11. Mix until glossy and smooth, matching the consistency of the vanilla icing.
12. Cover half of each cookie in a thin layer of vanilla icing, let it set.
13. Cover the other half with chocolate icing and let set.
14. Smooth over icing and let both sides of the frosting set completely before enjoying!

Taryn's Black & White Cookies

Adapted from Preppy KItchen

On Grief

Dayna said she could use more writing on grief; and I thought, "What do I know about grief?" This shouldn't have been a hard question for me to answer. My father died nine months ago, so I should be familiar with grief. Apparently, I haven't had a good understanding of grief and I'm still learning what it is. I lost other loved ones before my dad, but at those times I had a responsibility to be "The Strong One." Because of this, I suppose I never grieved in the way I think I should have. In my experience, loss and grief are something that other people go through, and I'm on the outskirts. I would feel sadness for the loss, and I would hurt from seeing the pain of the people I cared about, but I always needed to make sure that everything was still taken care of. I wasn't given, nor did I take, the space or time to allow myself to internally process those losses. Losing my dad changed this for me. I was no longer able to be, or expected to be, "The Strong One" who kept everything under control. I had to make some decisions, but otherwise, I had no choice but to lean on others while I mourned and came to terms with my new reality.

The strange thing is, now that I am reflecting back on my grieving process, I'm noticing how much I have grown and improved upon myself throughout it. I've learned about relinquishing control and trusting others. I've learned a lot more about who I am, and who I want to be, as well as who the people in my life are, and who I want in my life. Seeing life through this new lens of loss, I feel like I've been granted a whole new perspective on everything. A lot of the things that I thought I valued or I thought defined "me" were stripped away, because they no longer mattered or fit who I was becoming. Who I was, who I thought I'd be, who I can be, who I should've been... it all came into question for me. It's been unnerving to go through what feels like an identity crisis, but at the same time, I now have this opportunity to pick up all these pieces, and put them back together in an intentional way.

Grief has shown me that I can get through anything, but not only by relying on my own strength. Instead, it's also okay to be vulnerable sometimes and trust in the amazing people in my life. It's shown me that those who I've lost are not only with me in spirit, but also in the parts of me that they contributed to while they were here. It's taught me to identify and cherish those pieces they left behind with me. Grief reminded me that nothing is permanent, but that is a good thing, because we can reinvent ourselves whenever we want to.

I've been learning the kind of life I want to live, and the kind of legacy I want to leave behind. When I die, I want the people I've left behind to have this kind of clarity and see it as an opportunity to look at all the beautiful things in their lives. An opportunity to look at themselves the way that I see them, and learn to love all the parts of themselves that they maybe didn't appreciate before. Like those that I have loved and lost did for me, I want my legacy to inspire in my loved ones the desire to bring the best version of themselves forward. I'm learning how to live my life in such a way to make these things true. I still don't feel like I know much about grief, but I'm learning and I'm growing and I'm going to be fine.

Ingredients
-2 tablespoons yeast
-½ cup warm water
-1 cup milk
-8 tablespoons butter
-9 cups all-purpose flour (add an extra cup or two if needed)
-2 teaspoons salt
-7 eggs (6 for recipe, 1 for glaze)
-1 ½ cups sugar

Directions

1. Preheat the oven to 350°F.
2. In a bowl, stir yeast into water to dissolve. Let sit for about 5-10 minutes or when small bubbles begin to form.
3. In a saucepan, add milk and butter, bring to a simmer and remove from heat.
4. Combine flour with salt and set aside.
5. In a stand mixer, beat 6 eggs with sugar until pale and foamy.
6. Beat in milk mixture.
7. Beat in yeast mixture.
8. Begin to add flour to the egg mixture, beating constantly until dough forms and continue on medium speed for five minutes. If the dough becomes too heavy for the mixer, you can use a wooden spoon.
9. Turn dough onto a floured surface and knead with lightly floured hands; add flour as needed. Knead for about five minutes or until it is smooth and elastic.
10. Place dough in a lightly oiled bowl, cover with a cloth and let rise in a warm place until doubled (about two hours).
11. Punch down the dough, cover and set aside again until doubled (about 90 minutes).
12. Lightly grease three 8-inch cake pans.
13. Transfer the dough to a lightly floured surface and knead about three times, squeezing out air bubbles.
14. Divide dough into three loaves (about 1 ¾ pounds each) and shape into three large rounds.
15. Transfer to cake pans.
16. Cover the loaves with a towel and set aside in a warm place until they rise slightly, about 30 minutes.
17. Brush with egg glaze (1 egg white mixed with water) and make a 3-inch-long x ¼-inch-deep slit across the top with a serrated knife.
18. Bake for 50-55 minutes or until the internal temperature reaches 200°F.
19. Set loaves to cool completely before enjoying.

Krystal's Portuguese Sweet Bread

Adapted from Emril Website

Not All Bread is Sweet: A story of shattered perfection

Content Warning: Anxiety

Here I am, a thirty-year-old woman who once seemed to live the perfect life, surrounded by the perfect family.

I am the youngest of three children born to immigrant parents. My father immigrated to America at the age of twenty-three in the late 1970s, while my mother immigrated at the age of four in the mid-1960s. They met and got married in 1981, and soon they had my brother in 1982, my sister in 1985, and me in 1990.

Growing up, everything seemed perfect. My mom was a stay-at-home mom or worked school hours, and my dad was the primary breadwinner, leaving at four a.m. and returning at seven p.m. They worked hard so we could truly live the American Dream. We truly had nothing to complain about. My parents were extremely loving, caring, intelligent, and everything between. We could not have asked for better role models.

Were we spoiled? No, but we truly had it all, in every sense of the word—everything we ever needed.

My siblings and I had extremely close relationships with each other and my parents from childhood through adulthood. We truly enjoyed spending time together. I would visit my parents daily, make plans with my siblings multiple times a week, call and catch up multiple times a day. It was a perfect life... Until it wasn't.

Once we all grew up and began our lives, things became complicated, but our relationships did not change.

My sister was the first to marry and have children. She has two beautiful children and was married for nearly ten years.

My brother married about eight years after my sister, welcomed a child about two years later, and has another on the way.

I married a year after my brother, not yet having any children of my own.

So here we were, three siblings all happily married, starting our own lives and families, and my parents couldn't have been more proud. Their American Dream was coming true before their eyes.

I understand that my sister went through a tragic part of her life. I understand that the effects on her are far beyond mine, but I also think it is important to remember that the effects of divorce go past the husband, wife, and children.

The arguments and stress led to my newfound anxiety also spiraling. My roots, morals, and dignity were challenged every single day. Where was that loving family I was always surrounded by? What did I do wrong? Why was I being targeted?

Sometimes I feel like maybe I am the bad guy. Maybe I should just see what I see and keep my mouth shut. Maybe I should ignore it all and pretend like nothing ever happened. Maybe I should stop trying to help. Maybe I should stop caring.

The tears I have cried and the multiple anxiety attacks that have ensued over the last two years are all new to me. The feeling of my chest tightening and the feeling of the emotions physically creeping up through my body is terrifying. I feel the tears well up in my eyes without any idea why. I still wake up in the middle of the night with my mind racing and my chest pounding. I feel as if I am fighting a demon, refusing to back down and allow me to get back to sleep.

--

It has been nearly two years since this all began. Nearly two years since my perfect family got ripped apart. Nearly two years of trying to navigate this new me.

Do I still have a sister? I guess so.
Do I see her? Extremely rarely.
Do we make plans together or talk? Never.
Do I know anything about her? Only what my parents occasionally share.

Do I see my parents often? Not even half as often as I did.
Is spending time with them enjoyable? There is definitely tension in the air.

Will it ever be the same? No.
Will I ever be the same? No, but I will be stronger than ever before.

My siblings and I would still talk daily, make plans weekly, and enjoy each other's company, even after marriage. Our significant others understood the relationships and quickly became part of the family. They too became part of the phone calls, the dinner plans, the heartfelt conversations, the laughs, and the forever memories.

But let's get back to my sister.

Nearly a month before her ten-year anniversary, she and her husband decided to divorce.

This was the beginning of the end.

Soon, that perfect family we knew quickly came crashing down. The idea of divorce crushed my parents and truly changed them and my sister forever.

My sister soon began a downward spiral full of lies, deceit, and slight neglect of her children was devastating to witness someone who had it all together quickly fall apart.
She wouldn't come home. She wouldn't answer her phone. She shut away the family almost completely.

What was worse? The wedge it drove between us all.

Within days, I soon saw the relationship I had with my sister shatter. No longer would she ca No longer would we talk. No longer would I see her children. No longer did I look at her the same way. What was she doing? Why was she rejecting help from those who love her most

Time and time again, I caught her in her lies. I fought with my parents, who naively believed every word she said. They turned on me, accusing me of starting unnecessary drama, and stating that I was ultimately "after my sister."

Why would I possibly be after someone who I loved so much? We were truly inseparable fo years! It wasn't that I was after her at all. I was incredibly worried about the person I quickl saw her becoming. I knew she would not reach out and admit she needed help, but I did ev erything in my power to try and help in any way that I could.

Somehow, it still turned to me. My sister pushed me away as hard as she possibly could, no matter which approach I tried. My parents, knowing her fragile state, and knowing that any thing they said could trigger her into a rage, took their pent-up emotions out on me. I lived twenty-eight years of my life with hardly any disagreement with my parents, nevermind ful on screaming matches, name-calling, and accusations. Never in my life have I felt so betray frustrated, or hurt.

Ingredients

-1 large ripe mango (cut and peeled)
-2 tablespoons lemon juice
-2 tablespoons butter
-⅓ cup brown sugar
-1 tablespoon water
-1 ⅓ cups flour
-⅔ cup granulated sugar
-2 teaspoons baking powder
-1 5-ounce can evaporated milk
-¼ cup vegetable shortening
-1 large egg
-1 teaspoon vanilla extract

Directions

1. Preheat the oven to 350°F.
2. Slice mango and place in a small bowl, pour lemon juice over slices and toss lightly; let stand for 15 minutes.
3. In a circular 9-inch baking pan, melt the butter and then stir in brown sugar and water.
4. Arrange mango slices on top of the butter and sugar mixture.
5. Combine flour, granulated sugar, and baking powder in a medium mixing bowl.
6. Add evaporated milk, vegetable shortening, egg, and vanilla extract to bowl and mix on low speed until combined.
7. After combined, mix on medium speed for one minute.
8. Slowly pour and evenly spread out the batter over mango slices.
9. Bake for 30-35 minutes and let cool.
10. To unfold, run a small knife around the top of the cake to loosen and invert; serve warm or at room temperature.

Reinna Kani's Mango Upside-Down Cake

Adapted from VeryBestBaking

Story

Colorful stairs stretching down to a world unknown. Wings spreading in the sky amongst the winds. These are the stories that I have lived, that I have seen, heard, felt, tasted, and smelled. These are the stories that have saved my life. Before them, I lived in a world of darkness. If the journey of growing up is the delicate growth of a flower, then she was the cruel mindless child that picked it before it bloomed. And then, I was alone. I was alone with open wounds, and I believed it was only right that I twisted the knife further into my soul with the desire to end the torture of the breeze against my blood. But stories stopped me. Their colorful words enticed me to put down the knife if only for a moment and read. And watch. And listen. And live.

With one book, I live.

Secrets of Droon. I can still smell the plastic-covered paper that surrounded the rich pages of the book, with the painted image of children running down magical stairs. It was handed to me by my teacher, despite the fact that it was above my level. For years and even today, I have struggled with reading out loud. It was always like the words from the page faded from existence the second my eyes reached out for them, but the faint trace of their meaning would be left and that's what I read. I would read a sentence with practically the same meaning, but they wouldn't be the words on the page. This was always frustrating to me because the words that I was saying were my reality. They were what I truly saw, but everyone around me said I was crazy. To them my reality was false, but they couldn't tell me why. They never tested me to find the underlying reason. They never told me why I read slower than the other kids. They never told me why my eyes couldn't move on to the next line with ease. They never told me why even the numbers on my math sheet left me. I was just told that I was wrong, and I grew to despise reading because of it.

 Reading and school became the symbol in my life for everything that I was told to believe by her mindless cruelty: that I was worthless, that I was a waste of life, that I was pathetic, that I should just kill myself. I believed it, because what first grader can't read? And why would a first grader think otherwise, when that's all they've heard. But this book changed that for me. It was different. It wasn't about the life of some girl who faced her bully like the other books I'd been given. They only served to remind me that I couldn't stop the one in my own home. This book was about the destiny of two worlds weaving together four children for adventure and fun. It was beautiful. It was my escape. It was my salvation.

I live today because of that story and every one that followed after. Stories have come to consume the expanses of my mind and time. I don't just read or watch or listen to a story.

I imagine every outcome, every dynamic, everything I can, following my encounter with it. Stories have become a comfort to me when I feel broken by the weight of what I am. They've provided me with something to do, to cope with the stress of school and life. But most importantly, stories allow me to step away from myself—to put my heart into the chest of these characters and try to breathe the air they breathe, to cry their tears, to smile with them. In those moments, I don't feel broken. And I can feel at peace.

Mental health can be a battle every day, a battle you might not always win, and a struggle you might have to deal with for the rest of your life. And that's okay. Each person who is dyslexic, neurodivergent, depressed, anxious, traumatized, suicidal, or anything else, is a work of art. Sometimes marred and scarred by the world that is beyond their control, but they are masterpieces nonetheless. Art is something you pour your time and energy into, for sometimes years, before you ever believe it's close to being finished. Don't feel you have to paint every day, or even paint over what the world has done to you. Sometimes the scars are too deep to paint with, or you can't find it in yourself to even lift the brush. Just know that if what you have at the end of the day is not your masterpiece, you can always keep working. And it is okay to find your peace between the battles.

Stories have been my peace and I hope this one can help you find yours.

BIO

My name is Reinna Brummett-Swayze. I am a child of two races, without one. I am from a city that I was not born to. I have loved men and women, but people ask me to choose one. I am dyslexic. I am neurodivergent. I am depressed. I am anxious. I am all of these things in one. And yet most days I feel like I've been broken into many. I am only still standing because of the friends I've found in recent years. Baking is one of the ways I show my love to others and take time to focus on something else, when everything else feels like too much. This is one of the recipes that I have made for the people in my life that have helped me make it this far. I've dedicated this work to them: the teachers, friends, and families I've made, that saved me. I hope hearing my story can help others feel less alone, like these people did for me.

Ingredients

-1 egg
-2 tablespoons whole milk
-1 ½ teaspoons vanilla extract
-2 ¼ cup all-purpose flour
-½ teaspoon salt
-1 teaspoon baking soda
-1 cup unsalted butter, room temperature
-¾ cup white sugar
-¾ cup brown sugar
-2 cups semisweet chocolate chips

Directions

1. Preheat the oven to 375°F.
2. Whisk to combine egg, milk, and vanilla; set aside and let warm to room temperature.
3. In a separate bowl, sift together flour, salt, and baking soda; set aside.
4. Cream together butter and sugars on medium-high speed until the mixture resembles a batter.
5. Reduce speed and add egg mixture.
6. Gradually increase speed and mix until well-combined.
7. Slowly add the flour mixture and then stir in the chocolate chips.
8. Using an ice cream scoop, scoop out dough and line on parchment paper or greased pan.
9. Bake for about 10 minutes or until the edges begin to brown.
10. Remove from the oven and let cool for about 5 minutes, then enjoy!

Anita's Chocolate Chip Cookies

Adapted from WideOpen Hearts

Story

January 2020
Sounds of Truth
Anita Cellucci

You lost
Your way
Pain seeped in all
of our things
The windows, the floors, the house
All creaked and moaned
Emotions that poured from your being
Do you remember?
The way you walked
The room and the air moved faster
I could breathe
A sigh of relief
When you left

I wept
No one understood
The crying sounded
As if mirrors cracked
Cracking drove nails into the memories
All too soon
All because
You carried it like precious cargo
Someone might steal away

Lies to truth
Truth to lies
Remind us of our place
The fragility of it all
Lies roll off the tongue as if
Wax built up over generations
Only now has just begun to
Form a solid
Slowly and meticulously
Scraped with trepidation from each

Of our tongues
We attempt to become in tune with the
Melodic sounds
Sounds—

A mother enabling
A father
Pushing a daughter
To journey beyond the intended
I stand strong
This knowing
Nearby buzz of intent
The lasting sound of impact

Silence falls, a new day dawns
And the lies
Are no longer the truth
But the large black trash
Set to the curb
On Friday mornings

November 2020
Anita Cellucci
Heart Beating Reflection
My heart beating like
The slow tapping of the blinker
My car
as bumps
Make me hear thoughts of concern
Say no to the overthought
Our demands of the system
While the sounds of voices
Echo again and again

Doors closing while
Another opens
Opportunity awaits, deep
Reflections the mirrors that I pass
Distracted conversations of other days

All at once I am flooded
by the to-do list
The checked-off items
Never seeming to vanish
Neverending cerebral rush
Responsibility

If only days
began
Slowly breathe
In and out
Stopping to notice
The roses, the thorns

Sweet reflection and
The illusive resolution
Often hit with force
The decisions
Doing—not being

In the winter cold, icy
Darkness
Often light filtering
Begins
Ray of warmth
I am humbled
Human, human-ness
Breaks us all
Brake, Pause
Pause, reflect
My heart center
Grounding energy

BIO

Anita Cellucci is an educator, school librarian, writer, poet, and artist. As an observer of humans and life, she is vulnerable, courageous, and empathetic. She continuously looks for gaps and cracks in life and then dives deep to offer pathways to help students. If she is being honest, she often does this for family and friends, too. A practice of meditation, mindfulness, and yoga help to keep Anita grounded.

Self-Care Strategies

Self-care looks different for everyone, and just like coping skills and tools, there is no one-size-fits-all approach; rather, it is anything that re-energizes you! Over the years, self-care has been reclaimed. What used to only be thought of as bubble baths and manicures now has a broader definition. Self-care doesn't have to be extravagant—nor is it selfish. In fact, the best way you can care for others is by caring for yourself first. It also can be helpful to practice self-care consistently, not just in the moment.

Here are some of our favorite self-care suggestions:

- Ordering a subscription box from Find Your/Self Boxes
- Working on laundry, homework, or completing work tasks—checking something off your list
- Taking a nap
- Cooking or baking
- Moving your body in a way that feels good
- Going to therapy
- Using a weighted blanket
- Taking a long bath or shower
- Reading
- Shopping
- Listening to a podcast or music that you love
- Crafting, crocheting, embroidering
- Taking a walk in nature without headphones, just listening to your surroundings
- Being around people you love
- Playing a board game or video game
- Meditating or focusing on your breathing
- Writing or journaling
- Talking or writing a letter to a friend
- Going to see a movie or play
- Lighting a candle or using other aromatherapy
- Coloring or drawing
- Working on a puzzle
- Hiking or camping outdoors
- Taking photos
- Snuggling with a pet
- Self-care dance parties

Food for Thought and Soul

Author's Voice:

It would be hard for my younger self to believe that Bake it Till You Make it LLC exists. Not because I would have ever doubted myself as an entrepreneur; I have been creating organizations since elementary school. Rather, she would be surprised that food and baking are the art in which I chose to tell my story.

Growing up in an eating disordered household, it is hard for me to even believe I found myself here, as food for most of my life was really only associated with shame, not joy. However, after I realized the unifying power of food and the way I could expand its healing properties to deconstructing mental health stigma, I never looked back. This is why it felt very important to include a chapter dedicated to the power of food and baking, not only for self-care, but how it can transcend to nourishing the soul.

Ingredients

-1 and ½ graham cracker crumbs (10 sheets of graham crackers)
-5 tablespoons unsalted butter, melted
-¼ cup granulated sugar
- 4 8-ounce cream cheese blocks
-1 cup granulated sugar
-1 cup sour cream
-1 teaspoon pure vanilla
-2 teaspoons fresh lemon juice
-3 large eggs
-Optional: fresh fruit, whipped cream, other desired toppings

Directions

1. Preheat the oven 350°F.
2. Using a food processor, begin to make the crust and pulse graham crackers into fine crumbs.
3. Pour crumbs in a medium bowl and stir in sugar and melted butter until combined.
4. Press this sandy mixture firmly into the bottom of a 9-inch pan, no need to grease.
5. Pre-bake for 8 minutes.
6. Remove from the oven and place the pan on aluminum foil. The foil will wrap around the pan for a water bath in a future step. Allow the crust to cool.
7. To make filling, use a mixer to beat the cream cheese and granulated sugar together in a bowl until smooth and creamy.
8. Add the sour cream, vanilla extract and lemon juice and beat until combined.
9. On medium speed, add the eggs one at a time, and stop mixing after the final egg is incorporated in the batter; avoid overmixing.
10. For the water bath, boil a pot of water; you need one inch of water for the pan.
11. As the water is heating up, wrap aluminum foil around the pan.
12. Pour cheesecake batter on top of crust and smooth into an even layer with a spatula.
13. Place the pan in a large roasting pan and carefully pour the hot water inside of the pan and place in the oven.
14. Bake for 55-70 minutes and ensure the center is mostly set.
15. When done, turn the oven off and open the oven door slightly. Let the cheesecake sit in the oven in the water bath as it cools down for 1 hour.
16. Remove from the oven and water bath; cool cheesecake completely uncovered at room temperature.
17. Then cover and refrigerate for at least four hours.
18. Use a knife to loosen the cheesecake and slice for serving. Add any desired toppings and store in the refrigerator for up to 5 days.

Alysa's Cheesecake

Adapted from Sally's Baking Addiction

Story

Starting with the gender binary, there are many "black and white" ways of thinking that need to be deconstructed. In several areas of our lives, we are told things are one way or the other: "right or wrong," "good or bad," "this or that." And the more I recognize the binaries that are present in our world, the more I realize how deeply ingrained they are in the way I see myself.

I am always telling myself: I must be hard-working, I must be kind, I must be knowledgeable, I must be strong. And while these are all arguably good ways of being, expecting myself to be all of them all the time doesn't support my authenticity. Some days I need to relax rather than work full steam ahead. Sometimes I need to be honest even if it doesn't feel kind at the moment. Sometimes I need to be humble in my learning and be okay with saying, "I don't know." Sometimes, as my therapist taught me, I may feel more wobbly than strong. This patient and holistic view of myself has allowed me to find peace and self-love in more challenging moments.

In addition to helping heal my own self-image, I have recognized this approach of non-binary thinking can foster community and help build relationships. When we assign labels to others, we teach ourselves to only see them that one way. As a personal example, I used to view my parents' divorce as the fault of one parent, and not the other. This caused resentment between me and my mom. It also impacted other relationships, as I saw my dad as a victim, and my eventual step-dad as a co-conspirator. As an adult, I've learned how both of my parents are imperfect people and that sometimes, a "failed" relationship can help more beautiful connections come to fruition. Also, seeing my parents as whole people helps me be more patient and understanding of myself as an ever-changing and growing person. This is especially important as we move away from the strict roles of "parent" and "child" and we build more reciprocal relationships.

When we see life and ourselves in these ultimatums, we miss out on the shades of complexity that make our lives interesting and beautiful. Just like with this cheesecake recipe, you can do all the steps perfectly, and you may just end up with the perfect cheesecake. Or, like me, you may choose to take your own approach (there was no way I was letting it sit uneaten for 6 hours!). And your cheesecake might not be perfect but it will still be delicious, which is the goal (unless of course you are having Gordon Ramsey over for dinner, then you might follow the recipe to a T). So, as you bake this cheesecake, cut corners, find patience in your creativity, and focus on the joy of the process, not just the goal. I still struggle with this every day, but I am working on seeing myself as a whole, complex, imperfect person. The further I get in that journey, the more beautiful I find all parts of me, even the messy ones.

BIO

Alysa is a dedicated family member, avid try-er of new things, and video game enthusiast. She is currently working as an educator with a nationwide non-profit. She is confident and silly, active and adventurous, and the most frequent list writer. She plans to continue growing with the communities around her.

Ingredients

-2 cups all-purpose flour (and a bit more flour for the surface where you will be working the dough)
-½ cup granulated sugar
-2 ½ teaspoons baking powder
-½ teaspoon salt
-2 teaspoons orange zest (about 1 orange)
-½ cup unsalted butter, frozen
-½ cup heavy cream
-1 large egg
-1 teaspoon vanilla extract
-1 cup frozen cranberries
-1 tablespoon heavy cream
-1 tablespoon coarse sugar
- 1 cup confectioners' sugar
-2-3 tablespoons fresh orange juice

Directions

1. Whisk flour, sugar, baking powder, salt, and orange zest together in a large bowl.
2. Using a box grater, grate frozen butter and add it to the flour mixture and combine with two forks until the mixture comes together in crumbs.
3. Place in the fridge or freezer while mixing wet ingredients.
4. Whisk ½ cup heavy cream, egg, and vanilla extract together in a bowl.
5. Retrieve dry ingredients from fridge or freezer and drizzle over flour mixture while adding the cranberries; mix everything together until moistened.
6. Pour dough onto the counter and with floured hands, work the dough into a ball. It will be sticky, so add more flour if you need. If it seems too dry, add heavy cream.
7. Cut into 8 wedges.
8. Brush scones with tablespoon of heavy cream and sprinkle with coarse sugar.
9. Place scones on a baking sheet and refrigerate for at least 15 minutes.
10. Preheat the oven to 400°F.
11. Retrieve scones from the fridge and bake for 22-25 minutes or until golden brown around the edges.
12. Once out of the oven, let cool and make glaze by whisking confectioners' sugar and orange juice together. Add more confectioners' sugar to thicken glaze or more juice to thin; once at your desired consistency, drizzle over scones.
13. Scones will be available to enjoy for two days at room temperature or for five days in the refrigerator.

Allee's Glazed Cranberry & Orange Scones

Adapted from Sally's Baking Addiction

Story

The world is such a big place, why limit yourself?

What was once my travel mantra has now become more like a life mantra. At twenty-nine years old, I have come to learn that my love for travel goes beyond the experience of trying new food, learning about new cultures, seeing new landscapes, and experiencing new ways of life. Rather, traveling gives me a window into the way I see myself. It has been a vessel for me to build my own confidence and identity.

Growing up, I undeniably had middle-child syndrome. While I loved the aspect of having both an older and younger sister, I have been known to overcompensate a bit for any time I may have felt left out in my family, and ever since then, I have been searching for my "niche." Attending school and living in a big city opened my eyes to aspects of diversity I may have not had otherwise, but it was not hard to feel lost at times. Even when I attended college at Boston University, I recognized the yearning for something more. I had (and still have) incredibly close friendships and memories from my time in college, but I do wish I had been more confident in putting myself out there. I am not sure why, but nothing really called to me at the time. I look back now and see so much of my confidence has come with age. I have always been strongly opinionated and strong-willed, but for many years I kept this to myself. There was not one turning point for me, rather there were several steps in my journey to get here. Certainly, my professional life and working at Girls Inc. helped me grow, but also exploring the world helped me become proud of who I am. While I know it may sound counterintuitive, the more I travel, the more at home I feel in myself.

As I enter my thirties (in a year!), I am not sure what is next for me, but I want to make sure I do not limit myself when it comes to my adventures (both in travel and self-exploratory). Just like in explorations of new places, there is so much to still be uncovered and I look forward to what is next.

Ingredients

-1 cup dark chocolate chips
-½ cup butter (1 stick), plus one tablespoon for your pan
-1 cup white sugar
-½ cup light brown sugar
-3 eggs
-¼ teaspoon salt
-1 teaspoon vanilla extract
-½ cup all-purpose flour
-¼ cup of cocoa powder

Directions

1. Preheat the oven to 350°F.
2. Lightly brush a 9x9-inch pan with melted tablespoon of butter.
3. Melt ½ cup of butter and dark chocolate in the microwave for thirty seconds at a time and stir repeatedly until smooth and creamy. Once everything is melted, set aside.
4. In a separate bowl, add white sugar, brown sugar, and one egg. Whisk to combine and re-peat this with the other 2 eggs, one at a time, until everything is creamy. Then, add your salt and vanilla.
5. Slowly pour the chocolate mixture into the sugar and egg mixture. Use a whisk to gently mix the batter.
6. After you have mixed the chocolate batter, sift in the flour and cocoa powder. Sifting helps create a delicate and smooth consistency. Mix well.
7. Bake at 350° for 30 minutes, then remove from the oven and let them cool for 15-20 minutes.

Melody's Dark Chocolate Fudge Brownies

Adapted from
Jessica Adler's Sweet & Savory Blog

Story

Control & consistency—two things I constantly crave in life. Throughout my life, I have struggled to relinquish control and rely on others. For me, this was a learned behavior that I am working on reversing. There have been so many times where I have felt let-down, hurt, or guilty when asking for help, even when I so desperately needed it. After a while, I stopped asking for help and even now, it is hard for me to do. I am re-learning how to ask for help and how to recognize what I can control, and what I can't. And one thing I can control is this damn good brownie recipe.

Cooking and baking have taught me patience, flexibility, and how to release emotions in a healthy way. Simply put, baking is something I can control (for the most part!). So when I put on my apron that says "No bitchin' in my kitchen" and throw my hair up in a messy bun, I know at that moment, I am in complete control. I lay out my ingredients on my tiny apartment counter, get my KitchenAid ready to go, and then I mix the ingredients one-by-one, until they have all blended together—the perfect consistency.

I have made this recipe about a dozen times at this point, and not once has it failed me. I stick to the recipe and if I'm feeling fancy, I'll add a little razzle dazzle of peanut butter sauce or melted white chocolate on the top. But for me, knowing this recipe is going to be delicious and messy makes me feel at ease. With so many uncertainties in life, it is crucial to have consistency, in one way or another. Find consistency everywhere in your life—that never-fail-brownie recipe, the movie that makes you feel at home, the places that bring you joy, and most importantly, find consistency in the people who never fail to make you feel wanted and loved.

BIO

Melody Gregory oversees an after-school program for middle school youth at Girls Inc. of Lynn. She uses her Master's in Counseling to support, advocate, and engage with at-risk youth. Mel loves to spend her free time hanging out with her husband, George, and their herd of guinea pigs! Some of her hobbies include cooking, crafting, and spending time outside.

Ingredients

-2 cooked sweet potatoes
-½ cup cocoa powder
-½ cup maple syrup
-1 cup peanut butter (or nut butter of your choice)
-1 cup chocolate chips

Directions

1. Preheat the oven to 350°F.
2. In a large bowl, mash two sweet potatoes.
3. Once mashed, add in cocoa powder, maple syrup, peanut butter, and chocolate chips; mixing together after each ingredient is added.
4. Pour batter into an 8x8-inch brownie pan.
5. Bake for 25 minutes at 350°F.
6. Let cool and enjoy.

Hannah's Sweet Potato Brownies

Self-Care is Eating Good Food

While the term "self-care" has become a buzzword in our society today, I have come to find self-care is more than just a trend; rather, it is necessary for both growth and healing.

This all began when I was trained in Youth Mental Health First Aid. Mental Health First Aid is a training program much like CPR; however, Mental Health First Aid teaches participants how to respond to a mental health crisis, rather than a physical one. I found it interesting that when I was trained in Mental Health First Aid, self-care was the last topic we covered and only did so briefly. In contrast, when I took an "Understanding Suicide" course in college, self-care was woven into the content of the whole semester. These different experiences of learning and discussing self-care helped me realize how individualized self-care is, and I needed to find out what it meant for me.

One thing I have found important in my own journey to defining self-care is that it is not something that is done just when I become overwhelmed or stressed, but rather it is a daily practice that I incorporate in my life, like a thread I weave into each day.

I have also found my self-care revolves around prioritizing my own happiness. This is hard for me, as I would also consider myself to be a people-pleaser. I am learning how to make choices for myself and accept that not everyone will be happy with those choices. I am learning how to set boundaries in order to focus on my needs and overall well-being. Each day, I am working towards these goals in hopes it will ultimately allow me to overthink and stress less.

I also practice self-care in more "traditional" ways, such as making my bed every morning to feel I have accomplished a task, as well as keeping my room and living space organized. I cook meals that make me feel good and use cooking as a time to take a break from whatever I may be doing. I practice yoga when I can and find time for mindfulness. Even if I have a short break in my day, I put my yoga mat out, play a calming playlist, and breathe, even if it is only for fifteen minutes.

Since investigating what self-care looks like for me, I have come to find it truly expands to every facet of my life. Self-care for me is eating good food, it is going out and enjoying myself. It is exploring and keeping adventure in my life, watching sunsets, and laughing with my friends. It is seeing my therapist, who I adore. It is taking care of my physical health by going on walks and runs.

Even with all of these examples, this is all fairly new. I have learned that everyone expresses themselves differently and that is okay. Prioritizing self-care took time, and I am still learning. Work at your own pace and make decisions that will benefit you, your mental health, you're your overall well-being. Self-care is more than the face mask every once in a while (although I do love a good face mask at night and a glass of wine!), so find what works for you. Self-care is whatever you make it.

BIO

Hannah Levine from Framingham, MA, is a senior social work major with a minor in civic engagement at Salem State University (SSU). She is a Civic Fellow at SSU and works in the Center for Civic Engagement as a Senior Program Assistant, where she has been involved in advocacy efforts relating to voter registration, mental health awareness, food insecurity, and more, as well as working with community partners in the North Shore area. Hannah was also a 2019-2020 Newman Civic Fellow through Campus Compact, as a representative for SSU. She works for Jewish Teen Initiative as their Peer Leadership Fellows Coordinator, where she works to help create a more inclusive and connected community through leading a relational-engagement-based fellowship, where teens work to engage more Jewish teens in Jewish life. During the summer going into her senior year, Hannah was the college intern for HereNow, a teen-led project of The Jewish Board that empowers teens to have the conversation around mental health, resilience, and inclusion through an online platform. Currently, Hannah is an intern at Essex County Community Organization—a multifaith network of over forty congregations and the North Shore Labor Council that works to create a world where everyone belongs, everyone can thrive, and we all have a say in the decisions that affect our lives. In her free time, Hannah enjoys being in nature, spending time with her friends and family, especially her twin brother, and enjoying delicious foods—both out at restaurants and cooking them at home.

Ingredients

- -¾ cup butter, softened
- -5 tablespoons sugar
- -2 cups all-purpose flour

Directions

1. Preheat the oven to 350°F.
2. In a large bowl, stir butter and 4 tablespoons of sugar until well blended.
3. Stir in flour to the mixture.
4. Roll out dough on a lightly floured surface and sprinkle with the remaining tablespoon of sugar.
5. Using a cookie cutter or knife, cut out small circles or shapes of your choice.
6. Place cookies on an ungreased cookie sheet, about ½ an inch apart.
7. Bake for 20 minutes.
8. Let cool and enjoy.

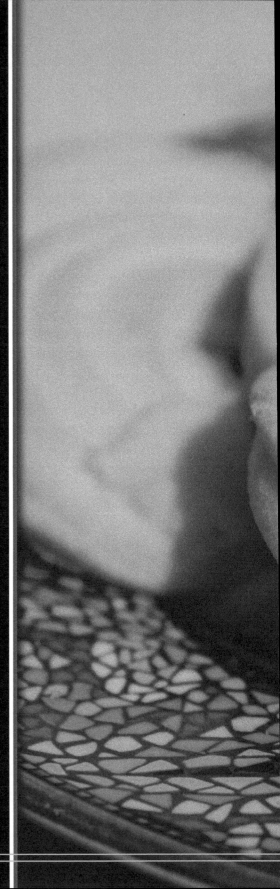

Brenna's Shortbread Cookies

Adapted from Betty Crocker

A Heart-to-Heart with Brenna Stewart

Q: How has mental health been a part of your life? How has it impacted you?

A: Personally, my mental health continues to be a non-linear process. Some days I feel I can conquer the world, while other days it can feel like quite the opposite, and that can feel scary and overwhelming. Over the years, my mental health has impacted my sense of self, my sense of worth, how I interact with others, and many other things—too many to list. It still does. However, over the years, my awareness of my own mental health and education around mental health in general has allowed me to become inspired and empowered to advocate for myself as well as others, and it has increased my overall empathy and compassion for situations similar and different to mine. I believe mental health is a spectrum and find the increased normalization of it in our society to be very important. Increased normalization means more support, and less shame, and I'm here for it.

Q: What are you passionate about and how has that influenced your well-being?

A: There are a lot of things I'm passionate about. As I get older, I'm learning more and more the importance of making space for those passions. I have always loved music, art, photography, running, and helping others. Whenever I dive into something I am passionate about, the best way to describe it is that I feel at peace. I've been on a journey for the past several years to align with my most authentic self, which I have found to be a very positive influence on my mental health.

Q: What would you say to someone who is struggling with their mental health?

A: Please don't give up. You can and *will* get through this with the right tools and support. I always encourage first slowing down in the capacity that works for you. A couple examples of this may look like breathing or drinking water; something simple that allows the mind to connect back to the body. This stems from a practice known as mindfulness. If you feel you don't have a foundation or tools to work with, I highly encourage seeking outside support in building this. This support can come from a mental health or other professional, or talking to a close friend or a family member. The current society we live in can make it extremely difficult to slow down, meet ourselves where we're at, and especially seek support without tying shame to it. In the midst of deep struggle, there can be so much paralyzing fear, so I believe that seeking comfort before solutions is okay. You don't have to be in a space for solutions when initially seeking help. Seek comfort, then solutions. One saying that I hear often and value greatly states: The only way out is through. I wholeheartedly believe this. As I continue on my healing journey, I am learning that patience with myself along with support from others is crucial in getting "through." You got this.

Ingredients

-2 cups flour
-1 cup dark brown sugar
-2 sticks butter
-½ cup white sugar
-1 teaspoon salt
-1 teaspoon baking powder
-1 teaspoon baking soda
-2 eggs (1 egg, 1 egg yolk)
-1 teaspoon vanilla extract
-2 cups roughly chopped Oreos
-½ cup dark chocolate chips
-½ cup white chocolate chips
-½ cup semi-sweet chocolate chips

Directions

1. Preheat the oven to 350°F.
2. In a medium sized bowl, whisk together the flour, baking powder, baking soda, and salt.
3. Whisk gently for thirty seconds and then set aside.
4. In a large bowl, cream together butter and sugar. Next, add the eggs and vanilla; mix together.
5. Slowly add the dry ingredients to the butter and sugar mixture in three separate stages.
6. Add the chocolate chips.
7. Stir in Oreo pieces with a wooden spoon or rubber spatula.
8. Put parchment paper down on a cookie sheet and separate dough into 2-inch balls.
9. Bake for 11-12 minutes.
10. Let cookies sit on the baking sheet after taking them out of the oven to allow for them to continue baking and to cool.

Brigid's Oreo Chip Cookies

Story

Content warning: Mention of an eating disorder

Baking has always been an escape for me. I remember when I was living in my childhood home and used to get stressed, I would stay up for hours baking cookies. So invested in the process, I didn't even realize how much time would go by.

When I was younger, I was diagnosed with an eating disorder. Back then, if you asked me if I had one, I would deny it. I was a super picky eater and *hated* when different foods touched on the plate. If they did, I would scream and cry and refuse to eat. This led me to stay at the same weight for several years, which was not healthy for me. Ultimately, I was put in a hospital for three months. That experience still haunts me and is not something anyone should have to go through so young.

Over ten years later, I still struggle with body image and food. Every day, though, I work to overcome old fears and celebrate when I feel stronger than before. I still do have more bad than good moments when it comes to this area of my life, but baking keeps my mind off of things. Like, there is nothing better than a cookie fresh out of the oven. The first bite always helps ground me, making me feel safe and warm. Bake by bake and day by day, I remind myself that I have come such a long way, and if that day is not going well for me, the next one is new.

I can confidently say I would not be the woman I am today without falling in love with baking. It is not only a beautiful art, but because of my culinary career, I have met the most amazing people and feel most at peace doing what I love.

I wish I could tell my younger self that everything would turn out okay, despite how hard life felt for me at the time. I wish I could have recognized then that the struggles and obstacles I faced would help me grow into the caring, loving, supportive, and strong person I am now. I wish I knew then that even though I never felt enough, being myself absolutely is. I wish I could tell her we will be okay, we are okay.

If I have learned anything from my journey, it is to always choose kindness; you never know who needs it and you never know where it will lead you.

BIO

Brigid Keating is a young professional currently living and working in Massachusetts. Originally from Fairfield, CT, she graduated from Lincoln Culinary Institute with a Baking and Pastries Degree. Outside her job as a baker, she loves to be outdoors and will take any excuse to go on a day trip to look in vintage shops. Her hobbies include baking, cooking, and personal photography.

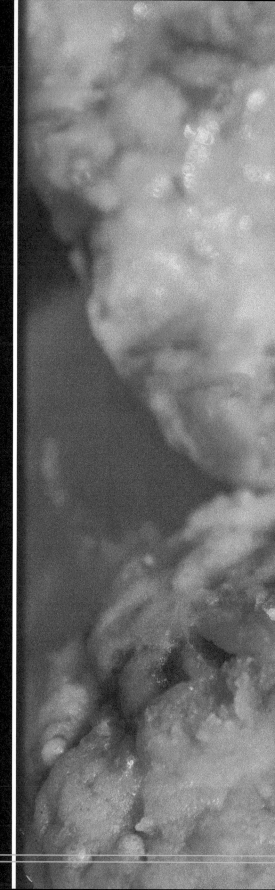

Ingredients

-1 stick butter
- ¾ cup sugar
-1 egg
-1 teaspoon vanilla extract
-⅓ cup sour cream
-1 ¾ cups flour
-⅓ teaspoon cream of tartar
-½ tablespoon corn starch
-½ teaspoon baking powder
-½ teaspoon baking soda
-2 cups rainbow sprinkles

Directions

1. Preheat the oven to 375°F.
2. In a large bowl, mix butter and sugar until creamy.
3. Add 1 egg, vanilla, and ⅓ cup sour cream.
4. Add 1 ¾ cups flour, ¼ teaspoon cream of tartar, ½ tablespoon corn starch, ½ teaspoon baking powder, and ½ teaspoon baking soda.
5. Add in sprinkles and mix.
6. Chill for at least one hour. Remove from the refrigerator, make dough balls and flatten.
7. Bake for 11 minutes and enjoy.

Lorin's Funfetti Cookies

Story

This time around, my story is not about me, but about my family.

As someone who has struggled with addiction and mental health, it was important for me to focus on the well-being of my children, especially during the pandemic.

If anything, the pandemic on a positive note allowed me to spend more quality time with my children. On the negative side, it really took a toll on both of my children—affecting their mental health in completely different ways.

My son had plenty of friends that he had contact with through video games and social media. He was motivated each day to stay in shape and did well in school. As the months turned into a year, his school work ethic and motivation began to diminish. He just started high school two months ago and it has been a struggle for him to climb back up to the top. There were so many decisions that needed to be made about his future regarding classes, pursuing music, activities, and socially fitting in.

Fast-forward to today... He is an amazing kid—sensitive and kind. He is a strong soul who has made a lot of life decisions, for which I'm so proud of him. He is doing well in school, has a lot of friends, and even has his first girlfriend. He has a bright future ahead.

My daughter, on the other hand, had a much harder time, having very few friends, connections, and missing the social aspect of school during these isolating times. She was depressed, couldn't focus during online school, was moody, and used food and videos for comfort. It was a very hard time for all of us; watching her go through this struggle was heartbreaking. Over the past nine months, she has been seeing a therapist. What a difference it has made, and I'm so proud of her for asking for help and for embracing the process. She likes sharing her innermost thoughts with someone other than her two moms, and I can see her confidence building each and every day.

Fast-forward to today... My daughter is thriving in every direction. She has made a lot of new friends in middle school, doing well in her classes, trying different after-school activities, and I'm incredibly proud of her. We are working on her mental and physical health each day and she is smiling, laughing, and passionate about so many things, including crystals and photography. She is beautiful inside and out, and her future also looks bright.

I am most proud of myself for recognizing that my children needed help and I wasn't ashamed to seek it out in any way I could. It is an ongoing effort for all of us, but a challenge I embrace every day, in hopes that my children grow up as happy, kind, appreciative human beings.

I have learned that parenthood is not all fun, games, laughter, and joy. There are so many ups and downs that you need to be able to navigate. The levels of emotions are incredibly deep and will bring forth unconditional love and a bond that lasts a lifetime. Despite the difficulties, it is definitely worth it!

Ingredients

-1 can sweetened condensed milk
-4 tablespoons cocoa powder, sifted
-2 tablespoons butter, plus as needed for rolling into balls
-A pinch of salt
-Toasted almond for the top

Directions

1. In a small saucepan, mix the sweetened con-densed milk, cocoa powder, salt, and butter.
2. Bring the saucepan to the stove and heat it over medium-low heat until it thickens. Mix often when on the stove to avoid it burning.
3. Run a wooden spoon (or spatula) in the mid-dle of the mixture to ensure it has cooked. The best way to tell if it is cooked is if the mix-ture takes a while to move once the spoon is run through the middle.
4. Take the mixture off the stove and let it cool to room temperature.
5. Once cooled, grease your hands with butter and roll into small balls (half a tablespoon)
6. Add a toasted almond to the top of the ball and enjoy.

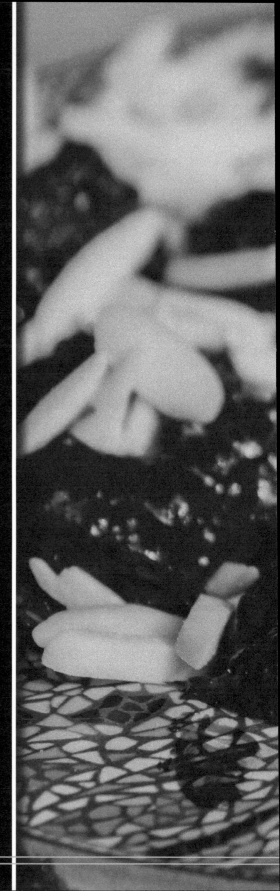

Montserrat's Brigaderos

Story

Content warning: Loss, grief

To Love Someone

To love someone profoundly is to live.

Without love you cannot live.

To lose one you love so deeply can feel like you should have never loved. The immense pain you feel can sometimes make you regret having loved at all because it hurts so deeply. But when you really take the time to reflect, you realize it hurt so much because the love was so profound.

My grandmother was like a second mother to me; I lost her in March of 2021 and stayed at her side until she passed.

Walking into the facility to visit her never got easier. Every time I left, I sobbed like a child but would wait until I turned the corner out of her sight. I would take a deep breath and try not to cry—it never worked. I did not care who was around and who would see me; I was in my own world. I just wanted to steal her away with me and give her her youth back, her memory, mobility, independence, and the feeling of being the matriarch of the family. I wanted to steal her away and bring her back to Spain with her family, where she was surrounded by love and familiarity. But I was helpless and I could not give her anything that I thought would make her feel comfortable or make her feel any less abandoned. Even though my family and I had no other choice, every time I would get ready to leave the facility, she would ask me to take her home. Knowing I was not able to and having to tell her I couldn't crushed my soul.

After losing her, in an attempt to move on and begin to overcome the feelings of this deep loss, I started to think about everything she taught me. Like the big heart she possessed that she passed on to me. The heart I use to try to help heal others and the way I try to understand humans on a deeper level (I have both her and my mother to thank for that).

I feel like she is with me every time I interact with a child, host someone at my home, smile at them and make their day... her smile was known everywhere. You could feel her warmth through her smile, so much so everyone would comment on it. She didn't speak English, and yet, when she would smile at people so invitingly, they would attempt to interact with her. So she would just put up her hands and smile bigger while she said, "No English." This only allowed for the other person to smile right back at her genuinely. So every time my smile becomes contagious, I think of her. I think of her when I think about how far being kind has gotten me in life and how my interactions with people have shaped who I am and the opportunities that have come to me because of this kindness... I have her to thank for that as well. You can imagine, the list of things she gave me is quite long! So when I feel sad and I miss her, I try to imagine what my life would be like if she hadn't been in it, and then I realize how blessed I am to have had her for all the years I did.

So when someone you love so deeply passes away and tears come to your eyes, think of the love that you shared that still encompasses you. Think about the connection you had with them that was so special and acknowledge that it is why it hurts so much. Be thankful for the time you had with them and recognize the pieces of them you carry with you that have now become a part of who you are.

There is no timeframe with grief. It could be years later and something reminds you of them... so share that memory. Allow their memory to stay alive in those moments, both for the people who knew the person and even those who did not. Always hold onto what you learned from them and pass on the memory of the one you loved so profoundly.

Thank You so much for taking the time to read A Unifying Blend: A compilation of recipes and stories to celebrate all that makes us human

Enjoyed this book and want to learn more about it?

The Organization: Bake it Till You Make it LLC is a community-based organization dedicated to destigmatizing mental illness, normalizing mental health conversation, and promoting authentic healing and recovery. Bake it Till You Make it LLC seeks to connect people through food, making "difficult conversation" more palatable, natural, and—in turn—commonplace, by using creativity, connection, and community.

Previous Work by Bake it Til You Make it LLC includes:

Bake it Till You Make it: Breaking Bread, Building Resilience (Award-Winning Cookbook, 2019): The first-of-its-kind mental health and resilience cookbook that tells the inspirational and resilient stories of over forty people, from all different backgrounds, who have overcome major life challenges. Each story is accompanied by a baking recipe chosen by the contributor. The book features mental health resource pages, complete with a self-care guide and information on how to become a mental health ally. The book has since inspired a movement to destigmatize mental illness and create a space to encourage vulnerability and authenticity to connect us all.

Bake it Till You Make it: Live!: A one-hour program facilitated by mental health activist and mental health cookbook author, Dayna Altman. Dayna tells the story of her mental health lived experience and the healing she has found through advocacy, specifically in creating the first-of-its-kind mental health and resilience cookbook, *Bake it Till You Make it: Breaking Bread, Building Resilience*. Dayna uniquely weaves her story through a demonstration as she bakes two recipes from her cookbook. Dayna uses ingredients as metaphors to guide her talk. She also brings up members of the audience to share pieces of their own stories as they work through the recipes together.

From the Kitchen: A stage adaptation of *Bake it Till You Make it*, bringing several stories from the book in a vignette-style play told through a cooking show.

Mix, Melt, Mend: Owning my Story & Finding my Freedom (Memoir, 2020): The authentic account of the journey of Dayna Altman. Dayna, a mental health advocate, is the creator of Bake it Till You Make it LLC, which published the first-of-its-kind mental health and resilience cookbook, *Bake it Till You Make it: Breaking Bread, Building Resilience.* In *Mix, Melt, Mend*, Dayna tells her own story in the framework of a cake pop recipe.

Beyond Measure Bakery by Bake it Till You Make it LLC: On a mission to make mental health conversation a "piece of cake," Beyond Measure Bakery combines boxes of baked goods and vetted resources to educate and empower the community to better understand mental health. This bakery believes in vulnerable conversation, an authentic lifestyle, and that sprinkles belong on everything.

Beyond Measure: The Podcast: A project that explores authentic storytelling, purpose, and vulnerability with community leaders, local role models, and everyday individuals who share their journeys to finding "their worth is beyond measure." Inspired by Beyond Measure Bakery by Bake it Till You Make it LLC, this podcast is a space to explore meaning, motivation, and community along with a love of baked goods.

Ways to Get in Touch:

Email: bakeitcookbook@gmail.com
Website: www.bakeittillyoumakeit.co
Instagram: @bakeittillyoumakeitllc
TikTok: @bakeittillyoumakeitllc
Facebook: Bake it Till You Make it: Breaking Bread, Building Resilience

About the Author

Dayna Altman is an energetic and dynamic entrepreneur, author, and creator. The full force and sole operator of Bake it Till You Make it LLC, Dayna harvests her passion for mental health advocacy by using food and baking to create an authentic recipe for vulnerable storytelling. A dual graduate of Northeastern University and an active Boston community member, Dayna has experience both working in the mental health field and with youth-based non-profits. Currently, Dayna works at a national education non-profit, and in all other hours of the day, she pursues public speaking, writing cookbooks, documentary filmmaking, and exploring new ways to change the world using her own story. Living with depression and OCD, as well as being in recovery from an eating disorder and sexual assault, Dayna Altman truly lives her message.

CPSIA information can be obtained
at www.ICGtesting.com
Printed in the USA
BVHW011358060522
636067BV00002B/3